1/93

Animals Around the World

ROBIN KERROD

PRENTICE HALL

New York   London   Toronto   Sydney   Tokyo   Singapore

ANIMALS AROUND THE WORLD

Managing Editor: Lionel Bender
Art Editor: Ben White
Text Editor: Angela Royston
Assistant Editor: Madeleine Samuel
Project Editor: Graham Bateman
Production: Clive Sparling

Media conversion and typesetting
Peter MacDonald and Partners and
Brian Blackmore

AN ANDROMEDA BOOK

Devised and produced by:
Andromeda Oxford Ltd
11–15 The Vineyard
Abingdon
Oxfordshire OX14 3PX
England

Prepared by Lionheart Books

Library of Congress Catalog Card
Number: 91-66997

ISBN 0-13-033382-4

Published in North America by:
Prentice Hall General Reference
15 Columbus Circle
New York, New York 10023

PRENTICE HALL and colophon are
registered trademarks of Simon &
Schuster, Inc.

Origination by Alpha Reprographics
Ltd,
Harefield, Middx, England
Manufactured in Singapore

10 9 8 7 6 5 4 3 2 1

First Prentice Hall Edition

CONTENTS

INTRODUCTION............................5

GEOGRAPHY OF ANIMALS 6
TROPICAL RAIN FOREST 14
TEMPERATE RAIN FOREST..........18
TEMPERATE FOREST 20
BOREAL FOREST.........................24
SCRUBLAND 28
DESERT 32
SAVANNAH 38
PRAIRIE.......................................42
TUNDRA.......................................46
MOUNTAINS 50
RIVERS..54

PONDS AND LAKES......................58
FRESHWATER WETLAND.............62
SALTMARSH.................................66
MANGROVES................................68
SHORELINE 70
OCEANS 74
ISLANDS......................................80
FARMLAND 84
CITY AND TOWN..........................86

GLOSSARY 90
INDEX..92
FURTHER READING 96
ACKNOWLEDGMENTS.................96

INTRODUCTION

Ecology is the study of living things in relation to their surroundings. It examines why different types of animals and plants are found in different places and how they survive in those places. It investigates how animals and plants interact with one another and with the environment. The environment is very complex and includes both non-living and living things. Climate, availability of water and sunlight all influence what lives where. But so too do the numbers and types of micro-organisms, plants and plant- and meat-eating animals.

Ecologists – people who study ecology – examine the natural world at a number of levels. For example, they study whole populations of a single species, individuals of several species, communities of living things and large ecosystems that cover vast areas of continents and oceans. This book introduces the ideas and concepts of ecology which try to explain the world of nature. The first part of the book looks at the world distribution of different habitats and the different types of communities of living things. The second part looks at the wildlife of land habitats, from forests and deserts to grasslands and tundra. Next is a survey of aquatic habitats, including rivers, lakes, wetlands and oceans. Lastly, there is a section on artificial habitats – farmland, cities and towns.

Each article in this book is devoted to a specific aspect of the subject. The text starts with a short scene-setting story that highlights one or two of the topics described in the article. It then continues with details of the most interesting aspects, illustrating the discussion with specific examples. It also covers conservation and people's relationships with their fellow animals and, where relevant, with plants.

Within the main text and photo captions in each article, the common or everyday names of animals and plants are used. For species illustrated in major artworks but not described elsewhere, the common and scientific (Latin) names of species are given in the caption accompanying the artwork. The index, which provides easy access to text and illustrations, is set out in alphabetical order of common names and of animal and plant groupings with the scientific names of species shown in parentheses. A glossary provides definitions and short explanations of important technical terms used in the book. There is also a Further Reading list giving details of books for those who wish to take the subject further.

◄A swarm of Monarch butterflies (*Danaus plexippus*) migrate south in the fall from the Great Lakes region of Canada to Mexico, where they congregate in their millions on trees.

GEOGRAPHY OF ANIMALS

It was their first day of study in the Himalayas in central Asia. The two American field biologists were determined to locate their subjects, a pair of young Snow leopards. For the next month or two, the biologists were to study the behavior and habits of these big cats. Then they were to journey 1,900mi south to Malaysia to study the Clouded leopard. They hoped all this would shed some light on the life-style of the jaguar, a species they were trying to protect back home in Mexico and which is considered to be the American equivalent of the leopard in the Old World.

Few species other than humans and the animals they have introduced can be found all over the world. Each region of the world has its own characteristic, or typical, kinds of plant and animal. For example, only Australia has koalas, and only tropical Africa has gorillas. Only the Arctic has Polar bears; and only South America has capybaras. Why should the plants and animals that live in each region be so different?

One obvious reason is climate. Gorillas, for example, are used to an easy life in the hot, humid, tropical rain forests, where there is plenty of vegetation for them to eat. They could not survive on the Arctic tundra, where the climate gets bitterly cold and vegetation of any kind is hard to come by. On the other hand, the Polar bear has a thick coat and layers of insulating fat to help it combat sub-zero temperatures. This bear could not tolerate the tropical heat and humidity of the African rain forests.

But climate cannot be the only factor determining the distribution of animals around the globe, otherwise animals would live wherever the climate suited them. There would be Polar bears in Antarctica and gorillas in South America, India, South-east Asia and northern Australia. There would also be koalas in North America and Europe and capybaras in India.

ON THE MOVE

Clearly, other factors must affect the distribution of animals. The most important of these is the changing geography of the Earth. The shape and position of the great land masses are very different today from what they were in the past. The major force that has shaped the Earth's surface has been the gradual movement, or drifting, of the continents.

Continental drift over millions of years has pushed some continents apart and prevented recent species of plants and animals moving from one continent to another. Other continents have moved together, allowing animal species to move between them. By studying the way in which the continents have drifted over the ages, scientists can trace how the present distribution of animals across the globe has come about.

Another name for continental drift is plate tectonics. The process occurs because the Earth's crust is not one continuous layer, but is split up into a number of separate giant segments, or plates.

The land masses we call the continents sit on these plates. They are solid, but the rock beneath them is partly molten, and this allows them to move apart or together.

SEPARATE REGIONS

Drifting continents is one reason why different regions of the world have their own unique animal species. These species are said to be endemic to the regions, which are referred to as zoogeographic regions.

There are six main zoogeographic regions. Some are made up of a single

▲ **Typical animals of the six main zoogeographic regions of the world**
Palearctic/Nearctic: Red deer, or wapiti (*Cervus elaphus*) (1); Red fox (*Vulpes vulpes*) (2). Nearctic: pronghorn (*Antilocapra americana*) (3); Mountain beaver (*Aplodontia rufa*) (4). Neotropical: Woolly opossum (*Caluromys lanatus*) (5); jaguar (*Panthera onca*) (6); capybara (*Hydrochoerus hydrochaeris*) (7); Brown-throated three-toed sloth (*Bradypus variegatus*) (8); Brown capuchin (*Cebus apella*) (9). African: gorilla (*Gorilla gorilla*) (10); giraffe (*Giraffa camelopardalis*) (11); Ring-tailed lemur (*Lemur catta*) (12). Australian: Tasmanian

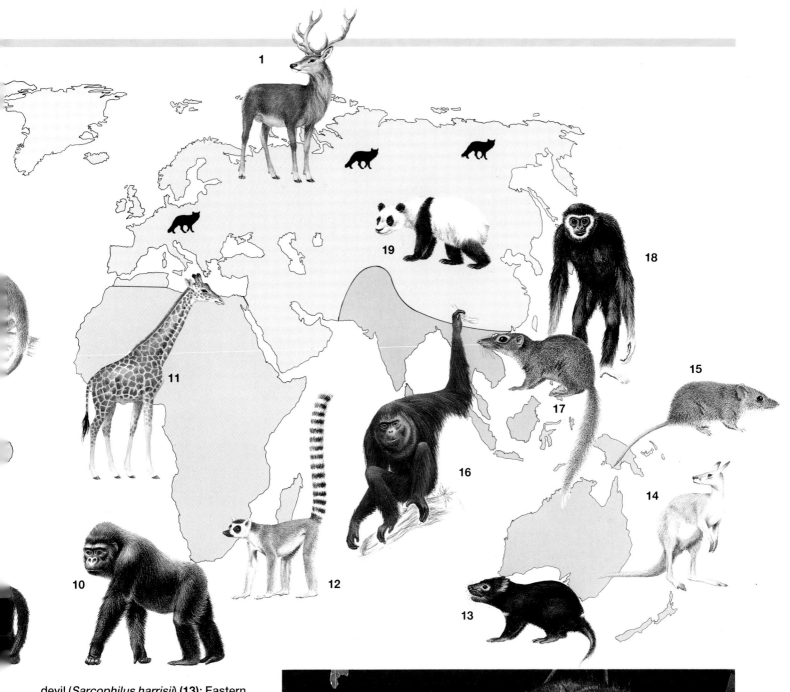

devil (*Sarcophilus harrisii*) **(13)**; Eastern gray kangaroo (*Macropus giganteus*) **(14)**; Brown antechinus (*Antechinus stuartii*) **(15)**. Oriental: orang-utan (*Pongo pygmaeus*) **(16)**; Terrestrial tree-shrew (*Lynogale tana*) **(17)**; Lar gibbon (*Hylobates lar*) **(18)**. Palearctic: Giant panda (*Ailuropoda melanoleuca*) **(19)**.

▶The Scaly-tailed possum is one of the rarer Australian marsupials. It uses its gripping, or prehensile, tail to grasp the branches as it travels through the trees. Like most nocturnal animals, it has large eyes to receive the maximum amount of light available in the dark.

continent. North America forms the Nearctic region; South America, the Neotropical region; Australia, the Australian region; and Africa, the African region. At one time or another all these continents have been more or less cut off from other land masses.

The huge continent of Eurasia (Europe and Asia) is split into two zoogeographic regions. The bulk of the continent forms the so-called Palearctic region, while India and South-east Asia together form the separate Oriental region. Deserts and the towering Himalayan mountain chain have isolated this region from the rest of Eurasia.

MARSUPIAL RULE
Australia has been almost totally isolated from other land masses since about 45 million years ago. At that time marsupials were the most advanced mammals. They give birth to small underdeveloped young, which then grow to maturity in a pouch.

In other regions marsupials eventually had to compete with placental mammals – those which give birth to large well-developed young. These are regarded as being more "advanced" because their offspring are able to fend for themselves at a younger age. In Australia, however, there was no such competition, and a great variety of marsupials – kangaroos, koalas, possums, and so on – evolved and flourished. Even more primitive egg-laying mammals survived, such as the Duck-billed platypus and echidnas.

Over 60 million years ago marsupials also lived in South America, the Neotropical region. But they are now represented on that continent only by the opossums.

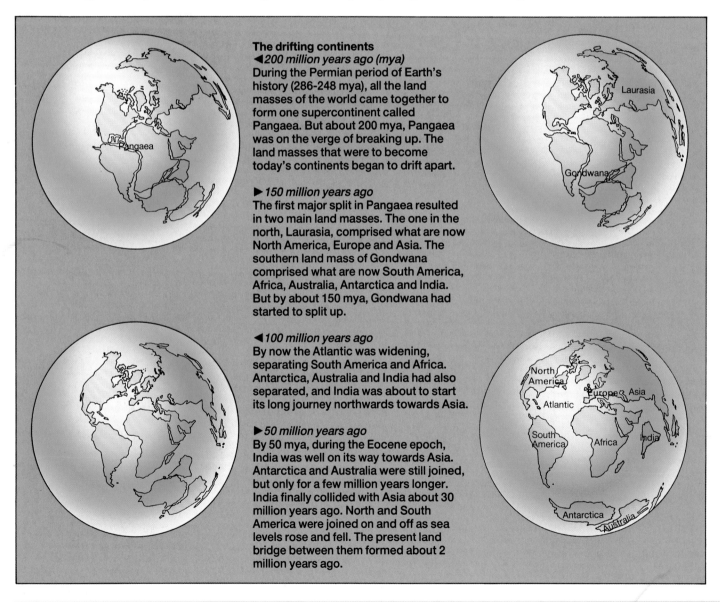

The drifting continents
◄ *200 million years ago (mya)*
During the Permian period of Earth's history (286-248 mya), all the land masses of the world came together to form one supercontinent called Pangaea. But about 200 mya, Pangaea was on the verge of breaking up. The land masses that were to become today's continents began to drift apart.

► *150 million years ago*
The first major split in Pangaea resulted in two main land masses. The one in the north, Laurasia, comprised what are now North America, Europe and Asia. The southern land mass of Gondwana comprised what are now South America, Africa, Australia, Antarctica and India. But by about 150 mya, Gondwana had started to split up.

◄ *100 million years ago*
By now the Atlantic was widening, separating South America and Africa. Antarctica, Australia and India had also separated, and India was about to start its long journey northwards towards Asia.

► *50 million years ago*
By 50 mya, during the Eocene epoch, India was well on its way towards Asia. Antarctica and Australia were still joined, but only for a few million years longer. India finally collided with Asia about 30 million years ago. North and South America were joined on and off as sea levels rose and fell. The present land bridge between them formed about 2 million years ago.

▼A Barrington land iguana suns itself on the rocks. It is one of the unique species endemic to the Galapagos Islands off the west coast of South America, which it colonized many years ago. The islands of Madagascar, Fiji and Tonga similarly have land iguanas found nowhere else in the world.

The marsupials did not evolve or thrive in South America because of competition with placental mammals such as anteaters and armadillos, and later with New World monkeys (howlers, spider monkeys and marmosets). (Historians refer to Eurasia and Africa as the Old World and the Americas as the New World, reflecting the order in which Europeans "discovered" them.) A variety of rodents, including porcupines and cavies (Guinea pigs), also entered South America with the monkeys. They came either from North America or from Africa.

Later still the present bridge of land with North America was formed, and a host of placental mammals, from weasels and foxes to jaguars and bears, flooded in. This led to the extinction of many unique endemic species such as the Giant sloth.

THE ATLANTIC DIVIDE
Many species of placental mammal appear to have evolved in North America, the Nearctic region. They were able at first to spread across Greenland into Europe, but that route became barred as the Atlantic became wider. Nevertheless, these mammals were still able to cross into Asia through Alaska and Siberia until the ice age became increasingly severe a few million years ago.

As a result, the animals of the Nearctic and Eurasia, or the Palearctic, are very much the same. Only the pronghorn and some rodents are unique to the Nearctic region. For the same reason the Palearctic region has only a few types of rodent and the unique Giant panda.

SAME BUT DIFFERENT
Among the early mammals to evolve in Africa – the African or Ethiopian region – were elephants, rhinoceroses and ancestors of the Old World monkeys and apes. These animals spread into the southern Palearctic region and India (the Oriental region). Many species in the Palearctic region eventually died out when the climate cooled down.

A barrier was set up between the African and Oriental regions by the onset of deserts in Arabia and the opening up of the Red Sea. Similar species in the regions have since evolved in a slightly different way.

This shows up, for example, in the differences between the African and the Indian elephant, the African White rhinoceros and the Javan rhinoceros, and the gorilla in Africa and the orang-utan in South-east Asia.

The Oriental region, comprising India and South-east Asia, is separated from the Palearctic by the Himalayas. This mountain range was formed when the plate carrying India collided with the main Eurasian plate about 30 million years ago. These mountains are so high and their climate is so severe, they have formed an effective barrier to the movement of animal species since then.

A LOT OF HOT AIR
Within the various zoogeographic regions of the world, climate is the main factor that affects where particular animals are to be found. Climate is largely produced by different parts of the world receiving different amounts of the Sun's energy. Because the Earth is round, the Sun's energy is concentrated more at the equator than at higher latitudes, that is at greater distances north and south of the equator.

This means that the climate is hottest at the equator and coldest at the poles. The temperature changes gradually from equatorial, to tropical, to warm temperate and cool temperate and then to cold at the poles.

The difference in temperature over the Earth sets the air circulating. As it is heated at the equator it rises. Then as it is cooled at the poles it drops. The hot air at the equator picks up moisture, which it sheds as it rises. So equatorial regions get a heavy rainfall. The now much drier air circulates to the poles and descends. It has little moisture left to shed.

WET AND DRY
Within this overall circulation are other smaller circulations. One of these creates descending dry air currents just north and south of the tropics (latitude about 30°). This often gives very dry, desert-like conditions at the surface. Farther north and south (latitude about 50° to 60°) is a disturbed region of rising and descending air currents, which usually give moist conditions at the surface. These are a feature of the temperate regions mentioned earlier.

▲The elephant evolved into two different species in Africa and Asia. The African species (above) is the larger and has bigger ears and longer, thicker tusks.

▶A savannah scene on the Serengeti Plains, Tanzania. This biome has been created by a variety of natural factors. For example, trees are scarce because of browsing by animals and the fires that occur naturally in the long dry seasons.

▼**Influencing the climate**
A beam of sunlight spreads over a greater area of surface away from the equator than a similar-sized beam on the equator (1). This means that temperatures become lower the farther away you are from the equator.

The main air circulation travels at high altitude from the equator to the poles and over the surface in the opposite direction (2). Other circulations take place in between. These circulations create regions of high and low pressure. If other factors except solar energy are ignored, there would be bands of different temperatures going from hot to cold away from the equator (3). Different climates produce a different mix of plant types, for example, rain forests in the tropics and tundra in the Arctic region.

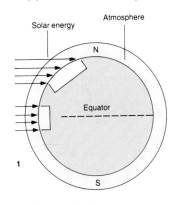

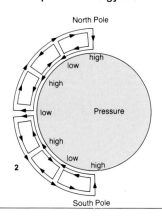

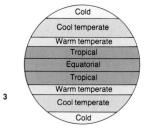

In practice the air circulation is complicated by the spinning of the Earth. This deflects the air currents at the surface – the winds – to the east (right) in the Northern hemisphere and to the west (left) in the Southern.

The direction of the winds blowing over the surface affects climate. When they blow in from the sea, they are usually moist and bring rain. When they blow over large expanses of land, they are usually dry and may give rise to drought conditions.

Among other factors that affect climate, the altitude, or height above sea level, is perhaps the most important. Temperatures fall increasingly the higher one goes above sea level. So cold climates can exist at the equator, if the altitude is high enough.

▼Polar bears prey on seals and walrus in the Arctic tundra. They build up layers of fat that carry them through a long winter of hibernation beneath the snow.

CLIMATE AND PLANT LIFE
The variety of different climates has led to the development of a wide variety of plants which can grow in each climatic region. In turn, these types of vegetation support particular types of animals.

Broadly speaking, there are about 10 different climatic regions, each with its own characteristic flora and fauna, or plant and animal life. The plants and animals form fairly distinct ecological units, called biomes.

The animal species that occupy the same kind of biome in different parts of the world are not necessarily identical. But they are often similar in the way they have learned to live in, or have adapted to, a particular environment. For example, the guanaco that grazes the South American grasslands, or pampas, is a similar kind of beast to the bison that grazes the prairie grasslands of North America.

1 Tropical rain forest
Canopy of several layers of trees
Colombo, Sri Lanka

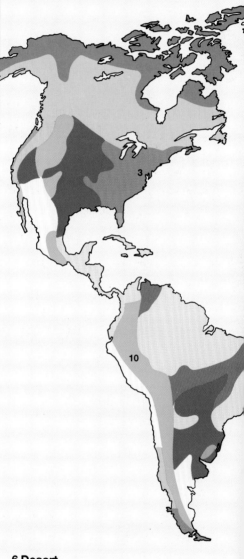

6 Desert
Well-spread low shrubs
Baghdad, Iraq

2 Temperate rain forest
High tree canopy, tree ferns underneath
Hobart, Tasmania

3 Temperate forest
Tree and shrub canopy, herb layer
Washington DC, USA

4 Boreal forest
Snow-shedding evergreen trees, shrubs
Verhoyansk, Siberia

5 Scrub
Evergreen trees/shrubs, or open grassland
Capetown, South Africa

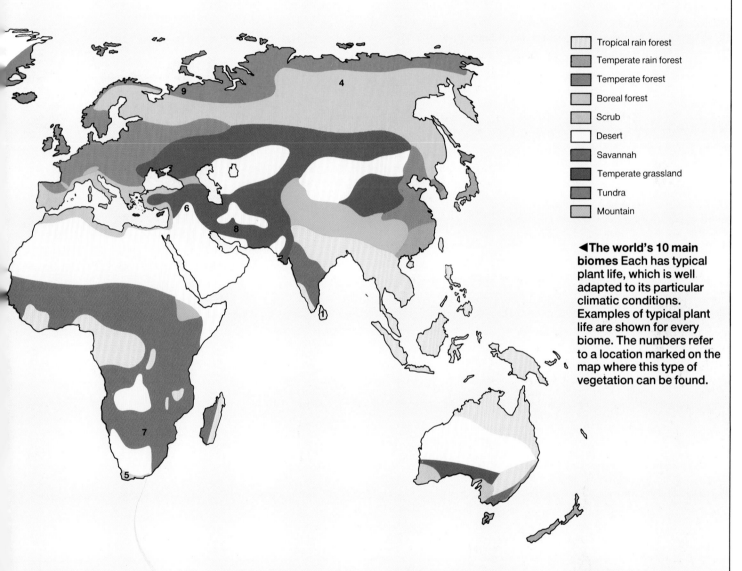

Tropical rain forest
Temperate rain forest
Temperate forest
Boreal forest
Scrub
Desert
Savannah
Temperate grassland
Tundra
Mountain

◄**The world's 10 main biomes** Each has typical plant life, which is well adapted to its particular climatic conditions. Examples of typical plant life are shown for every biome. The numbers refer to a location marked on the map where this type of vegetation can be found.

7 Savannah
Scattered trees and tall grass
Harare, Zimbabwe

8 Temperate grassland
Grass canopy
Kabul, Afghanistan

9 Tundra
Low cushion plants and dwarf shrubs
Archangel, Soviet Union

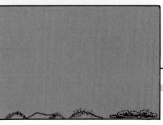

10 Mountains
Cushion plants or dwarf shrubs
Cuenca, South America

TROPICAL RAIN FOREST

A seething river of insects, up to 65ft wide, is scything a path through the leaf litter on the floor of the Amazon rain forest. It is a raiding party of army ants, containing up to 200,000 ferocious worker and soldier ants. It is unstoppable. The marauding ants are flushing out and killing anything that lives in the leaf litter – other ants, centipedes, cockroaches, spiders, even scorpions. The larger animals of the forest are running for their lives. If they get trapped by the ant swarm, they too will be killed.

Straddling the equator in Africa, the Americas and South-east Asia are regions that provide a great richness of plant and animal life. Their natural wealth is unequaled anywhere else in the world. They comprise the tropical rain forests.

The tropical rain forests thrive in equatorial regions, near the equator, and in the tropics, the region between the lines of latitude which are often

▲High up in the dense canopy of the Amazonian rain forest of South America, a howler monkey feeds on young leaves. Like all the New World monkeys, it has a prehensile, or grasping tail, which it uses to anchor itself while feeding.

referred to as the Tropic of Cancer (latitude 23½° north) and the Tropic of Capricorn (23½° south).

Rain falls on most days, and averages between 100 and 160in each year, depending on the location. Some places have been known to have as much as 400in of rainfall in a year!

▶In the rain forest of Panama, in Central America, a Brown-throated three-toed sloth perches in an emergent tree above the dense leafy canopy. The sloth can be thought of as a kind of "tree cow", since, like a cow, it has a many-chambered stomach which breaks down the cellulose in the leaves. Sloths do not extract much energy from this leafy diet, which accounts for their characteristic slowness of movement.

Temperatures in the tropical rain forest are fairly steady throughout the year and are between 68° and 82°F.

There are regions of forest north and south of the tropics that also have high rainfall. But they do not experience such high temperatures. They are called temperate rain forests (see page 18).

THE LAYERED FOREST
The tropical rain forest provides ideal conditions for plant growth – constant warmth and very high humidity (moisture). In undisturbed areas this growth tends to be arranged in a series of layers.

The dominant layer is the canopy. This is a dense mass of foliage formed by trees growing up to about 65ft tall. Breaking out of the canopy here and

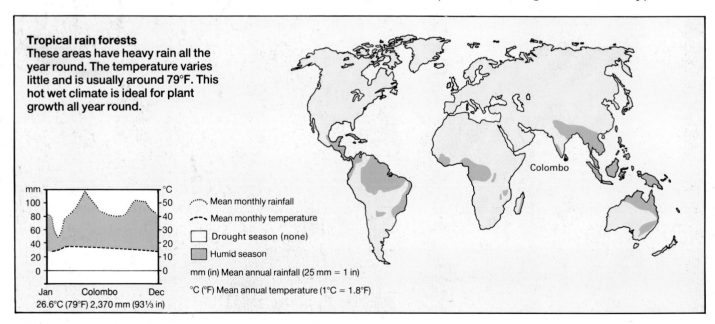

Tropical rain forests
These areas have heavy rain all the year round. The temperature varies little and is usually around 79°F. This hot wet climate is ideal for plant growth all year round.

····· Mean monthly rainfall
--- Mean monthly temperature
☐ Drought season (none)
▨ Humid season

mm (in) Mean annual rainfall (25 mm = 1 in)
°C (°F) Mean annual temperature (1°C = 1.8°F)

Jan   Colombo   Dec
26.6°C (79°F) 2,370 mm (93⅓ in)

Colombo

there are the taller emergents, trees up to 130ft tall. Beneath the canopy, middle and lower layers of "understorey" vegetation may also be found.

DARK JUNGLE

With such dense vegetation above blocking out the sunlight, the floor of the forest is dark with less growth than might be expected. Creepers abound, climbing the trunks and branches of the trees as they struggle to reach the daylight high above. These plants are epiphytes – they rely on other plants for support. Some epiphytes, including many beautiful orchids, root high up in the tree trunks and branches, taking nourishment from their host and from the air. Other flowering plants are saprophytes – they live on the decaying leaf litter that covers the forest floor in a thick carpet.

Where the forest canopy is broken, more light filters through to ground level, and the vegetation can become very dense. This produces the kind of impenetrable undergrowth usually associated with "jungle."

FOOD FOR ALL

The animal life in the tropical rain forest is rich and varied. There is a plentiful supply of food, as abundant rainfall and consistently high temperatures allow plants to flower, seed and fruit throughout the year. The forest floor and the various layers of foliage provide a wide range of habitats for many different animals.

▲ ▼ **Species of bat of the tropical rain forests of Panama** They feed on a variety of abundant food. The False vampire bat (*Vampyrum spectrum*) **(1)** is carnivorous. The Fringe-lipped bat (*Trachops cirrhosus*) **(2)** preys on frogs. The Mustache bat (*Pteronotus parnelli*) **(3)** is an insect-eater, while the Fishing bulldog bat (*Noctilio leporinus*) **(4)** catches fish.

The largest animals live on the forest floor. The elephant, tapir and gorilla all feed on the understorey vegetation. Other animals, such as the chevrotain in Africa and Asia and the agouti in South America, feed on the sparse ground cover.

LIFE IN THE UNDERSTOREY

The smaller beasts are preyed on by a variety of big cats, such as the jaguar in South America and the Clouded leopard in South-east Asia. These lithe carnivores climb into the branches of the understorey and pounce on their prey as it passes underneath. The cats also prey on birds and rodents. So do snakes, such as the highly venomous fer de lance and bushmaster.

The understorey supports a wide range of animals. Conditions on the forest floor are so wet that even frogs have taken to the trees. Tree frogs spawn and develop in the water that collects in plants or holes in the trees. Many are very poisonous and advertise this with their brilliant coloring.

Insects are found in vast numbers in the trees. Many have evolved remarkable protective coloration, or camouflage, and look like twigs and leaves. But the most spectacular insects of all are the butterflies, which are often dazzlingly beautiful. The many species of birds, such as parrots and macaws, are amazingly colorful, but they are all outshone by the birds of paradise of Papua New Guinea in their stunning courtship display.

IN THE CANOPY

Birds fly in and around the forest canopy, and mammals live there too. Monkeys travel through the canopy, often in noisy troops. Using their long arms and legs to good effect, they can swing along at a remarkable speed. The New World monkeys of South America have a prehensile tail, which they use as an extra limb when moving about and feeding in the branches. In South America the sloth is a canopy dweller too, though it is as slow as the monkeys are quick.

Up in the canopy the monkeys and sloths are out of reach of the big cats that roam far below. But they can be attacked from above by some of the world's largest birds of prey. These include the Harpy eagle in South America and the Crowned eagle in Africa. The eagles live in the emergent trees, swooping down into the canopy when they spot likely prey. Two species of fruit-eating birds with huge brightly colored beaks also live in the emergent trees of the rain forests – the toucan in South America and the hornbill in Africa and Asia.

▶A male Regent bowerbird displays at the elaborate bower it has built to attract the female (shown behind). As in many bird species, the male is brilliantly coloured, while the female is drab. The brilliance of the male helps him to attract a mate; the drabness of the female camouflages her while she is sitting on the nest incubating the eggs.

4

TEMPERATE RAIN FOREST

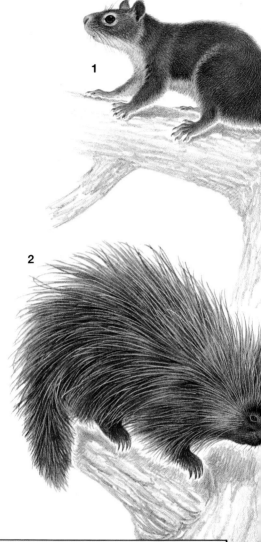

At night most of the birds in the New Zealand rain forest have gone to roost. But one, the size of a large chicken, is out foraging for food. It is a kiwi, which is probing into the deep litter with its long bill. Its small eyes are useless in the pitch darkness, and it has to find its prey by smell. A crashing sound in the undergrowth nearby alerts it, and it takes to its heels and runs fast in the opposite direction. It cannot escape by flying, because it has no wings or tail.

The relatively small regions of temperate rain forest, such as the homeland of the kiwi, occur just to the north of the tropics in the Northern hemisphere, and just to the south of the tropics in the Southern hemisphere.

The temperate rain forests have less rainfall than the tropical ones, but still an appreciable amount – between about 40in and 80in a year. The rainfall is much more seasonal than it is in the tropical forests, with most of it falling during the winter. The temperature is also lower than in the tropical forests, but there are seldom any winter frosts.

GIANT REDWOODS
The mild damp climate of the temperate rain forests is very favorable for plant growth. The typical trees are broad-leaved evergreens. In the rain forest regions in eastern North America there are evergreen oaks. Evergreen oaks and beeches are common in the temperate forests of Japan. Conifers also feature in Japan's forests, as they do in New Zealand.

By far the most impressive of the rain forest trees, however, are the Californian redwoods, which are among the tallest and oldest living things on Earth. They can reach heights of up to 330ft or more.

The temperate rain forests are not as structured, or layered, as the tropical

▶Some typical animals of a temperate rain forest in Washington State, USA Douglas squirrel (*Tamiasciurus douglasii*) **(1)**. North American porcupine (*Erethizon dorsatum*) **(2)**. Fisher (*Martes pennanti*) **(3)**. Black-tailed or Mule deer (*Odocoileus hemionus*) **(4)**. American shrew mole (*Neurotrichus gibbsi*) **(5)**. Similar types of animal are found in other temperate rain forest regions.

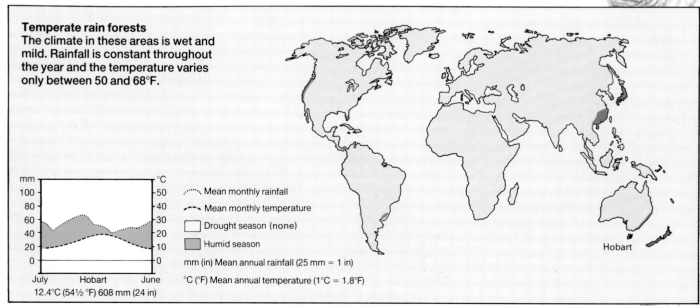

Temperate rain forests
The climate in these areas is wet and mild. Rainfall is constant throughout the year and the temperature varies only between 50 and 68°F.

······· Mean monthly rainfall

----- Mean monthly temperature

☐ Drought season (none)

▨ Humid season

mm (in) Mean annual rainfall (25 mm = 1 in)

°C (°F) Mean annual temperature (1°C = 1.8°F)

July   Hobart   June
12.4°C (54½ °F) 608 mm (24 in)

Hobart

▲A Great spotted kiwi foraging in the undergrowth of the temperate rain forest in the South Island of New Zealand.

ones, and there is much more leaf litter, dead branches and fallen trees cluttering up the forest floor. This is because the creatures that help decompose the fallen vegetation, such as woodlice and springtails, work more slowly in the cooler climate.

Despite the clutter on the forest floor, several large animals can often be found there. They include, in the North American forests, the Mule deer and the American black bear, which can also climb trees. They share the habitat with other mammals, such as moles and martens.

Similar kinds of animals are found in the temperate rain forests of other regions. For example, there are black bears in South America (where they are called Spectacled bears) and in Japan and China (where they are called Asian black bears).

QUOLLS AND KIWIS

The most unusual animal species of the temperate rain forests are found in New Zealand and Tasmania, where there are several unique marsupials, such as the Tasmanian tiger quoll. This is a carnivore that behaves rather like members of the cat family, climbing trees and preying on roosting birds. In Tasmania too lives the shy Red-bellied pademelon, a kind of wallaby.

The most unusual animal in the New Zealand forests is the country's national bird, the kiwi. There are three species, all of them are unable to fly.

Kiwis have only been able to survive in New Zealand because the islands have long been isolated by the sea, which has prevented invasion by predatory mammals. Only in comparatively recent times have kiwis come under threat, from the destruction of their forest habitat and from predators such as domestic cats, which were introduced by people.

TEMPERATE FOREST

For several weeks since the winter cold set in, the hedgehog has been sleeping in its cosy nest, lined with leaves and grass, in a hole in the side of a canal embankment. Today, however, the weather has turned particularly warm, and the hedgehog has woken up feeling hungry. Cautiously, it peeps out of its hole to see if the area is clear. It makes its way to a spot nearby where plants have started to grow again and where blackbirds are digging for earthworms. When it has eaten its fill of worms and slugs, it returns to the nest and soon sinks back into sleep.

The winter cold that the hedgehog experienced, when temperatures very often fall below freezing, is a feature of the temperate forest regions, which cover much of the eastern half of the United States and most of Europe.

The typical trees of the temperate forests are deciduous, that is, they shed all their leaves when the temperature drops in the fall. They then become dormant. Their tough bark helps them withstand the cold, which would kill anything growing. The buds, the points where new growth will start, are small and well protected. They burst into life in the spring, when the temperature begins to rise.

THE FLOWERS IN SPRING

The structure of the deciduous forest is a simple one. There is a canopy, up to about 100ft tall, and a lower shrub layer up to about 30ft tall. The canopy is usually relatively open, which lets in much more light than in a rain forest, and allows plenty of growth on the forest floor.

Most growth at ground level takes place in early spring, when the plants take advantage of the period before the leafy canopy of the trees fully develops. At this time many woods are carpeted with spring flowers.

RHYTHM OF THE SEASONS

The seasonal nature of plant growth in deciduous forests means that the supply of food available for animals is seasonal too. So, to survive, animals have to be generalists rather than specialists, which means that they must be able to live on a variety of

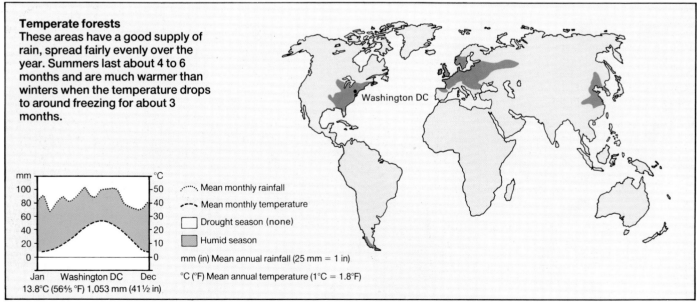

Temperate forests
These areas have a good supply of rain, spread fairly evenly over the year. Summers last about 4 to 6 months and are much warmer than winters when the temperature drops to around freezing for about 3 months.

Washington DC

mm ... Mean monthly rainfall
--- Mean monthly temperature
☐ Drought season (none)
▨ Humid season

mm (in) Mean annual rainfall (25 mm = 1 in)
°C (°F) Mean annual temperature (1°C = 1.8°F)

Jan   Washington DC   Dec
13.8°C (56⅘ °F) 1,053 mm (41½ in)

▲A hungry brood of Coal tits begs for food as a parent returns to the nest. Tits are among the most common birds in deciduous woodland, feeding mainly on insects, but also on seeds and berries. The Coal tit has an extensive range, breeding from the British Isles, across Europe and Asia, to Japan.

▲(Right) A Gray squirrel in its drey, or nest, in an oak tree. The Gray squirrel is a native of North America, and was introduced to Britain in 1876. It has become a major forest pest there, killing saplings and young trees by stripping off the bark.

▶Not oak apples but growths known as galls produced by the presence of the larvae of a gall wasp, *Biorrhiza pallida*, which feed inside. The life-cycle of many temperate forest insects includes such a tree-dwelling stage.

foods rather than on just one type. The other factor that limits the number of animal species in the temperate forests is the winter cold. Animals adopt different means of surviving. Some, such as many birds, migrate to warmer climates. The Willow warbler, for example, is a resident of many north European woodlands during spring and summer. But it flies 6,300mi to Africa for the winter.

THE WINTER SLEEP

Most animals cannot escape the cold in this way, however. Some, including hedgehogs and dormice, hibernate instead – they go into a deep winter sleep. Their body temperature drops very low and their heart beats only feebly. Like the trees around them they seem dead. For months they remain like this, their body feeding on an internal store of fat.

Squirrels and badgers also fall into a winter sleep, but it is not so deep, and their body temperature does not fall.

From time to time they wake up and feed if they can. Squirrels, for example, feed on nuts they have stored during the fall. They need to have many such stores because they do not remember where they all are.

FIGHT FOR SURVIVAL

The other animals of the forest survive as best they can during winter. Birds like tits search for insects and eggs in the bark of trees. Deer and wild pigs grub around in the leaf litter for roots and any remaining vegetation. They may also browse on bark and branches if no other food is available. A bitter winter will often result in trees being severely damaged or killed by browsing animals.

THE LEAF LITTER

The leaves that are shed in abundance in the fall are a major feature in the ecology of the temperate forest. They act as an insulating blanket for hibernating animals and plants alike. Little

breakdown (decomposition) takes place in the leafy layer in the winter. But in the spring woodlice, worms and smaller creatures get to work on the previous year's leaves.

The leaf litter becomes alive not only with the decomposers, but also with the creatures that prey on them, such as beetles and spiders. This varied animal life also makes rich pickings for moles, shrews and birds.

ABUZZ WITH INSECTS

Insect life within the temperate forests is rich and varied too. Moths and butterflies often survive the winter in the bark. Species that eat leaves lay their eggs so that they hatch as the buds begin to burst in the spring.

There are good reasons for doing this. For one thing the fresh leaves are rich in nitrogen, which the insect young need to build up their body proteins. Also, they do not yet contain toxic compounds, which might harm the young. Many old leaves tend to

▲A Eurasian badger foraging in the leaf litter on the forest floor for earthworms, insects and snails. It will also eat voles and mice. It is a nocturnal animal and spends the day in its burrow, called a sett.

▶A group of Red deer grazes in a forest glade. The male is distinguished by its fine set of antlers. Among all species of deer except reindeer, only the males have antlers. Every year they shed them, and grow new ones.

be low in nitrogen and high in tannin, which make them not so nice to eat.

The Spangle gall wasp has evolved an ingenious method of surviving the winter. It lays eggs on oak leaves, which causes them to develop galls, or growths. The young develop inside these galls, which fall off the leaf before the leaves themselves fall. The falling leaves then provide a covering layer to protect the young gall wasps.

◄Curled up in its nest, a Common dormouse sleeps throughout the cold winter. By curling up, it reduces the exposed area of its body, and so reduces heat loss.

▼A Japanese macaque foraging in the winter snow for food. The macaque is the only forest-dwelling monkey outside the tropics. It lives in the temperate forests of Japan, keeping mainly to the ground. It survives the winter cold by growing a thick furry coat.

BOREAL FOREST

In a northern pine forest of Canada a family of Red squirrels is sitting in the branches of a tree, feeding on seeds in the pine cones. One of the group sees their arch enemy, the goshawk, some distance away, and makes a chucking call to alert the others. One of the younger squirrels panics and jumps out on an exposed branch. The goshawk sees its chance and swoops down. Within seconds the young squirrel is struggling in the bird's vise-like talons, with no hope of escape. Within an hour it has been torn to pieces and swallowed.

The boreal, or northern pine, forests occupy vast regions of the Northern hemisphere. "Boreal" comes from the name Boreus, god of the north wind in Ancient Greece. No similar forest regions occur in the Southern hemisphere. The boreal forests merge in the south with temperate forests and grasslands, and in the north with the virtually treeless tundra.

Being at a higher latitude than the temperate forests, boreal forests have a much harsher climate. The summers are shorter and the winters much colder. Only about 2 months of the year are free from frost, and temperatures in some places may fall as low as −70°F at times.

THE CONE-BEARERS
Because the growing season is short, plants of boreal regions must be able to burst quickly into growth when

▲Beavers build dams with the trunks and branches of trees they cut down with their sharp teeth. They make the dams watertight by adding stones and mud. They also build their lodges of the same materials.

▶A Red squirrel eating a nut, which it holds in its forepaws. It is an attractive creature, with conspicuous ear tufts. It is one of the commonest residents of the boreal forests of Europe and Asia, where it is preyed upon by martens and goshawks.

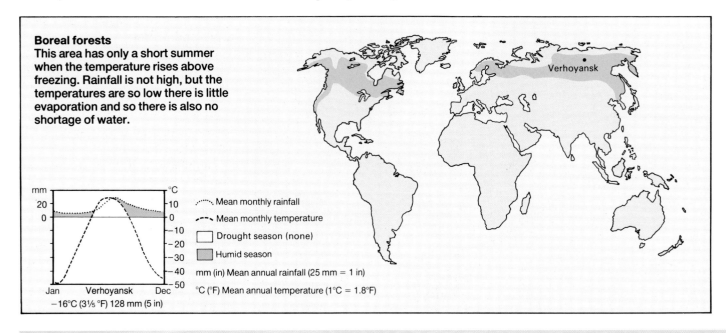

Boreal forests
This area has only a short summer when the temperature rises above freezing. Rainfall is not high, but the temperatures are so low there is little evaporation and so there is also no shortage of water.

Verhoyansk

.... Mean monthly rainfall

- - - Mean monthly temperature

Drought season (none)

Humid season

mm (in) Mean annual rainfall (25 mm = 1 in)

°C (°F) Mean annual temperature (1°C = 1.8°F)

Jan   Verhoyansk   Dec
−16°C (3⅕ °F) 128 mm (5 in)

▲A pair of Red crossbills, natives of the boreal forest regions of Europe and Asia. Only the males are red; the females are green. The bill of these birds crosses over at the tip. This enables them to open out the scales of cones and pick out the seeds.

temperatures start to rise in the spring. Evergreen plants with existing leaves can do this better than deciduous ones, which need time to develop their foliage. And that is why evergreens dominate the boreal forests. Among the deciduous trees that do grow in boreal regions are birch, aspen and willow.

The evergreens of the boreal forests are not broad-leaved evergreens like those in the rain forests. Broad leaves would lose too much heat. Boreal evergreens feature thin needle-like leaves, which lie close together and retain more heat.

The majority of the evergreens are conifers, or cone-bearing trees, such as pines, spruces and firs. Another feature of these trees is their shape, which is like a cone pointing upwards. This shape is very effective in shedding snow before it builds up enough weight to break the branches.

Compared with the forests farther south, there is not much variety in the plant life on the floor of boreal forests. This is almost certainly due to the recent geology of the region. The boreal regions occupy areas covered by glaciers until a few thousand years ago. There has not been enough time for a greater variety of plant species to become established since then. Indeed, there are still glaciers at high altitudes in the regions, for example, in North America and Scandinavia.

HUNTERS AND HUNTED

Among the larger animals of the boreal forests are the caribou, reindeer and moose, which graze on any available vegetation. Like most of the other mammals, they tend to remain in the forest during the winter months for protection against the icy winds and bitter cold. The feet of the reindeer and moose are specially adapted for life in the snow. They are splayed out to give a larger area over which to spread their weight.

Big as they are, these beasts are prey for an increasingly rare species, the wolf. Wolves hunt in packs for greater efficiency. They sometimes attack domesticated livestock, which has led to their being hunted by farmers and so to their dwindling number.

The boreal forests are also the home of many other predators, such as lynxes, foxes, martens and goshawks. Their prey includes particularly the Snowshoe hare and the Red squirrel.

BUSY BEAVERS

In the boreal forests in North America the American beaver has a marked effect on the vegetation, particularly around streams and rivers. The beavers feed on the bark of deciduous trees such as birch and aspen. They will often eat right round the trunks of the trees, thereby killing them.

Beavers also deliberately cut down trees, which they use to construct dams and build their lodges, or homes. They dam streams to make a pond with deep water, and then build their lodge

in it. The lodge is built so that the living area is above the water, but the entrance is underwater. This protects the beavers against such predators as the wolverine. During the fall the beavers store branches at the bottom of the pond, and then feed on these branches in the winter.

THE CROSSBILLS
Most of the birds that live in the boreal forests during the spring and summer migrate south in winter to warmer places where they can still find insects and other food. Exceptions are the birds of prey and the crossbills.

Crossbills are birds of the finch family, which have adapted to feed on conifer seeds, the most plentiful food supply in the boreal forest. They have a bill that crosses over at the tip, and they use this to pry open the tough cones that hold the seeds.

Insects, such as beetles and moths, thrive in the forests in the summer months. Over a period of time insect populations may build up in huge numbers. Their caterpillars, or larvae, feed on the leaves and can completely strip trees of foliage, and so kill them. Among the most destructive species is a moth called the Spruce budworm.

People are also affecting the character of the boreal forests, which are increasingly being harvested for their timber. The evergreen conifers yield softwood, used as sawn timber for construction and to make woodpulp for papermaking. Careful management will be needed in the future to prevent the eventual destruction of this unique biome.

◄**Examples of boreal forest animals**
The trees of the boreal forest offer animals some protection from the extreme cold of the northern winter. The elk, or wapiti (*Cervus elaphus*) **(1)**, a sub-species of Red deer, is one of the largest animals in boreal forests. The coat of the Snowshoe hare (*Lepus americanus*) **(2)** turns white in winter, which provides it with camouflage. In summer the coat turns gray-brown. The lynx (*Felis lynx*) **(3)** preys on the Snowshoe hare, as do foxes, coyotes and martens. In the air the Peregrine falcon (*Falco peregrinus*) **(4)** is a formidable predator.

SCRUBLAND

In the heart of the Mallee scrubland of southern Australia, the male Mallee fowl has been building a nest for some months. He has been collecting leaves at the nest site, and then covering them with soil. The nest has by now become a huge mound of rotting vegetation, rather like a compost heap, and, like a compost heap, it is warm inside. Now it is egg-laying time. The male scoops out a hollow in the mound, in which the female lays the eggs. She does not need to incubate the eggs – that is brought about by the heat of the mound. Eggs and chicks are then ignored.

The Australian scrubland, home of the Mallee fowl, covers many thousands of square miles. However, by far the largest area of scrub is found around the Mediterranean Sea, and so the type of climate enjoyed by this biome is often called Mediterranean. It has hot, dry summers and mild, wet winters. During the summer months the average temperature is often more than 78°F. In winter the temperature rarely falls to freezing point (32°F) and almost all of the annual rainfall of up to 20in occurs in the winter.

Low woody shrubs form the typical vegetation of the arid scrubland. The leaves of these plants are small and leathery. They are well adapted to

▲ The puma is sometimes known as a cougar or Mountain lion. It is the largest of the North American cats, with a head-and-body length up to nearly 6½ft. The puma ranges widely in search of its main prey, which are Mule deer and elk. But it will also take smaller prey, such as rodents. Like the other North American cats, the puma is now an endangered species.

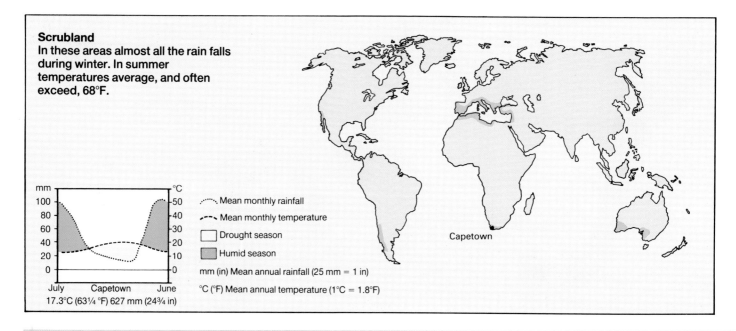

Scrubland
In these areas almost all the rain falls during winter. In summer temperatures average, and often exceed, 68°F.

..........: Mean monthly rainfall

- - - : Mean monthly temperature

☐ Drought season

▨ Humid season

mm (in) Mean annual rainfall (25 mm = 1 in)

°C (°F) Mean annual temperature (1°C = 1.8°F)

July   Capetown   June
17.3°C (63¼°F) 627 mm (24¾ in)

Capetown

▼Some animals of the Californian chaparral: The Antelope jackrabbit (*Lepus alleni*) **(1)**, noted for its speed; Merriam's kangaroo-rat (*Dipodomys merriomi*) **(2)**; Collared peccary (*Tayassu tajacu*) **(3)**, a small wild pig; the sidewinder (*Crotalus cerastes*) **(4)**; White-tailed antelope-squirrel (*Ammospermaphilus leucurus*) **(5)**; Western collared lizard (*Chrotaphytus collaris*) **(6)**; Road runner (*Geococcyx californianus*) **(7)**, with lizard prey.

withstand the blistering heat and drought conditions of summer. Some shrubs are evergreen and their leaves tend to shrivel in summer due to lack of water. Other shrubs minimize water loss by losing their leaves as the summer drought takes hold.

CHEMICAL WARFARE

Many of the shrubs are rich in strong-smelling oily chemicals, which stop insects and other animals from eating them. The oils also find their way into the surrounding soil, and prevent the growth of competing plant life. The California sagebrush is an example of this kind of shrub. The oils it contains are also inflammable. In the tinder-dry conditions of high summer the sage-brush easily catches fire, and the whole region is swept by fire on average about every 25 years.

Apart from the shrubs, the plant-life consists mainly of annuals and bulb plants. They burst into growth after the annual rains, flower and seed, and then die back during the summer. Interestingly, the seeds of many of the annuals are stimulated into growth by the drop in temperature in the late fall. This contrasts greatly with the typical seeds of temperate regions, which are triggered into growth by the warmth of spring.

THE WILD WEST

The area of scrubland in California where the sagebush is found is known as the chaparral. It is the home of a fascinating variety of wildlife, despite the harsh summer climate. The top carnivore of the chaparral is the beautiful but deadly puma. It preys on a variety of animals, from small rodents to the large Mule deer. It is active mainly at dusk. In some areas wolves and Grizzly bears are still to be found, although they are becoming scarce, as they increasingly come into conflict with people.

Ground squirrels live in burrows in the ground, as do the smaller kangaroo rats. Both store seeds in their burrows. The seeds probably help to conserve water by absorbing the moisture given out by the animals when they breathe.

Among bird life, the Road runner, or Chaparral cock, is the most distinctive. It does not fly well, but can run remarkably fast, hence its name. It feeds on lizards and small rodents. It is a member of the cuckoo family, but does not have the typical cuckoo habit of laying its eggs in another bird's nest. The chaparral was also part of the original home territory of the wild turkey, from which the domesticated variety descended.

LIFE IN THE MALLEE

Australia has two regions of scrubland, in western Australia and South Australia. In southern Australia it is called mallee. In some areas wallabies rest in the scrub during the daytime, but they feed during the night in more open grassland. Much of the scrubland region, however, is so dense that it is largely impenetrable by the larger mammals.

MATORRAL BURROWERS

The scrubland in Chile, in South America, is known as the matorral. Among this region's most interesting residents is the degu. It is a burrowing rodent about the size of a rat. It uses its sharp claws to dig for roots and tubers. It also eats some grasses and produces an interesting pattern in their distribution. It feeds on grasses that grow around its burrow, but it does not eat sneezeweed. So sneezeweed, which cannot compete with the other more vigorous grasses, thrives and grows only around degus' burrows.

MAQUIS AND GARRIGUE

The scrubland of the Mediterranean region is called maquis when it is thick and garrigue when it is sparse. There is scarcely any undisturbed scrub in this region because of the influence of the human population over thousands of years. Most areas are now cultivated and, with the help of irrigation, profitable crops are grown. Groves of olive trees have replaced scrub in many areas.

The wildlife of the region has also suffered because of human intervention. Herds of domesticated goats, kept for their meat, milk and hides, have been particularly destructive to the ecology of the region. They are able to eat virtually anything that grows, and even climb trees to browse on the leafy branches.

▶A male Mallee fowl looks after his incubation mound in which the female will lay her eggs. She lays between 5 and 33 eggs at intervals of several days. Mounds used year after year reach 16ft in diameter. The chicks hatch at any time from 50 to 90 days.

DESERT

Darkness has fallen over the sand dunes. The sand is now cool, and the air temperature is falling rapidly. Dotted about here and there are little black Tenebrionid beetles, standing on their head, with their abdomen pointing up in the air. This is not some curious mating ritual but an instinctive habit that enables the beetles to survive. As the air temperature falls further, moisture from the air slowly condenses on the beetles' bodies as dew. The water runs down into their mouths, and they drink.

Deserts are among the most forbidding places on Earth as far as life is concerned. They are hostile for two main reasons: the lack of water and the very high temperatures that last throughout the year.

Deserts are usually defined as places where the annual rainfall is less than 10in a year. But many deserts have an annual rainfall of less than 2in, and in some it may not rain for years at a time. In one part of the Atacama Desert in Chile, for example, it has not rained for over 400 years!

The daytime air temperature in the hot deserts rises to 120°F or more in the summer, and at such times the temperature of the surface can rise to 195°F, nearly the boiling point of water. Altogether deserts form one of the largest biomes of the world and occupy about one-eighth of the land surface. The largest desert region is the Sahara Desert of North Africa, which covers an area of over 3 million square miles – nearly as much as the United States.

▲A scorpion scurries over the sand in north-east Africa. It uses its large, menacing, pincer-like appendages to capture spiders and other scorpions to eat. Scorpions tend to hide in rock crevices and burrows in the sand.

▶A clutch of ostrich eggs starting to hatch in the Namib Desert in Namibia. The clutch will usually include eggs laid by a number of hens, though they will be incubated only by the "major" hen and its mate. The chicks are well developed when they hatch out and are able to run around and follow their parents to food and water shortly afterwards.

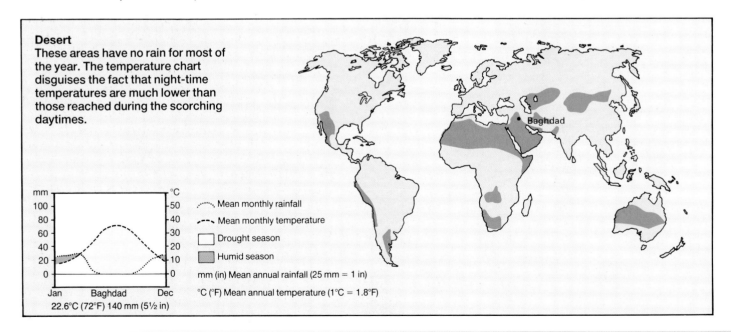

Desert
These areas have no rain for most of the year. The temperature chart disguises the fact that night-time temperatures are much lower than those reached during the scorching daytimes.

mm / °C
100 / 50
80 / 40
60 / 30
40 / 20
20 / 10
0 / 0
Jan Baghdad Dec
22.6°C (72°F) 140 mm (5½ in)

········ Mean monthly rainfall
– – – Mean monthly temperature
☐ Drought season
▨ Humid season
mm (in) Mean annual rainfall (25 mm = 1 in)
°C (°F) Mean annual temperature (1°C = 1.8°F)

▲This gecko in the Namib Desert has webbed feet, which stop it sinking into the sand and help it to dig its burrow. Geckos are a kind of lizard. Most are active at night and feed on insects.

▶A cactus plant with flower buds starting to open. Insects pollinate the flowers as they feed on nectar. A number of desert birds, such as owls, nest in holes in the thick stems of old cacti.

There are signs that the area of desert is increasing, partly because of a change in climate and partly because of too much grazing of the marginal areas by the livestock of nomadic farmers. Such desertification is occurring in other parts of the world too as the human population increases.

CACTI AND DESERT BLOOMS

It is astonishing that anything can live in the drought and high-temperature conditions of the hot deserts, but some plants and a surprising number of animals can. Various species of cactus are the typical plants of the deserts of the Americas. In the African deserts their place is taken by members of the euphorbia plant family, which have evolved along similar lines to the cactus.

Cacti are perennial plants that have become specially adapted to drought conditions. Their swollen, succulent stems are able to store water. The surface of these plants is shiny, so that it reflects much of the sunlight that falls on them.

Cacti have no real leaves so photosynthesis to make food takes place mainly in the stems, rather than in the leaves as in other plants. To photosynthesize, plants have to open their pores, or stomata, and take in carbon dioxide. Most plants do this during daytime but many species of cactus open their pores at night when the temperature is lower, and when they will lose less moisture.

Annual plants, those that live for just one season, are common in many deserts. They have evolved in such a way that they can take immediate advantage of any rain that falls. For much of the time they exist as seeds. When the rains come, they spring into rapid growth, flower and seed in just a few weeks before the drought sets in again. The abundant seed produced during this brief "flowering of the desert" is one of the major food sources for desert animal life.

DESERT RATS AND RELATIVES

Among the commonest animals in the deserts are rodents such as gerbils,

▼A deadly predator in the desert is the desert viper. It submerges itself in the sand with only its eyes visible above the surface (below). It digs its way into the sand by means of specially adapted scales on the body (bottom). As it wriggles, the scales scoop out the sand and deposit it over its body. This species is the Common sand viper, pictured in the Negev Desert in Israel.

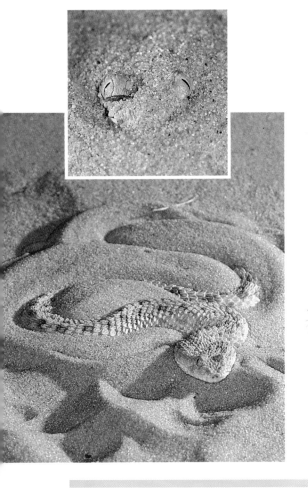

1

▲A scorpion devouring its grasshopper prey. They usually paralyse their prey by stinging with their tail, which is arched over the body.

▼**Some desert mammals** The African porcupine (*Hystrix cristata*) **(1)**. The Cape ground squirrel (*Xerus inaurus*) **(2)**, from South Africa. The Marsupial mole (*Notoryctes typhlops*) **(3)**, from Australia. The Fennec fox (*Vulpes zerda*) **(4)**, from North Africa and the Middle East.

kangaroo rats, pocket mice, jerboas and ground squirrels. They feed on seeds and grasses; some eat insects as well. Being small creatures, these animals quickly heat up when they are exposed to the Sun. For this reason most of them spend the daytime in burrows they have dug below the ground where they are protected from the worst heat.

Kangaroo rats, jerboas and some other small rodents never drink water. They get the water they need from the food they eat. It is produced from carbohydrates as their food is digested. Their bodies also reduce the amount of water lost by producing very concentrated urine.

DESERT CARNIVORES

The rodents are important prey for the various carnivores that live in the desert. Among those that live on the edge of the desert are members of the cat family, such as the caracal in Africa and Asia, and the puma in North America; and members of the dog family, for example the Striped hyena in Africa and Asia, and the dingo in Australia.

Among the smaller carnivores are various reptiles, such as lizards and

snakes; and arachnids, such as scorpions and spiders. Many of these animals are venomous. The Gila monster of the western United States and Mexico is a venomous lizard; while the rattlesnake is one of the most dangerous poisonous snakes.

There is a good reason why desert predators should be able to deal a deadly blow. In the desert, food is relatively scarce, so when a predator comes across a suitable prey, it must make sure of killing it quickly. In general the carnivores need little to drink. They get most of the water they need from the bodies of their prey.

BIRD LIFE

Various birds are present in desert regions. Being airborne, they can travel long distances between water holes, roosting places, nests and feeding grounds. Birds in general have a higher body temperature than other animals, and so can tolerate the desert heat better.

Among desert birds are various hawks, eagles and vultures, which feed largely on carrion. Among these predatory birds is the Egyptian vulture, which is well known for its habit of dropping stones onto ostrich eggs to break their thick shells.

The ostrich is probably the best-known bird of the African deserts. It is a huge bird, up to 8ft high. It can run at speeds of up to 30mph on its long, powerful legs. Its large size is an advantage in the desert because the larger the mass of an animal, the longer it takes to heat up. Large flightless birds similar to the ostrich

◄The Shingle-backed lizard of the Australian deserts is slow-moving and cannot escape from predators by running away. Instead it puts on an impressive threat display to frighten them. It opens it mouth wide to show its strong jaws, and pokes out its long blue tongue, hissing all the while. Note how well its body is camouflaged for the desert terrain.

are found in some other deserts, for example, the emu in Australia.

SHIPS OF THE DESERT

The large size of the other well-known desert-dweller, the camel, gives it the same advantage. In addition the camel has adapted to desert life in other ways. It can go for several days without drinking, using water stored in its body.

The camel is able to lose more than a quarter of its body weight of water without coming to any harm. It is also able to drink large quantities of water very quickly to make good this loss – as much as 30 gallons in 10 minutes. Donkeys have the same capability of existing for days without water and then drinking rapidly. This is why they are widely used as animals for carrying goods in hot climates.

KEEPING COOL

Camels and donkeys, together with sheep and goats, are to some extent insulated from the heat by their hairy coats. This acts just as well as a barrier against heat as it does against cold.

These animals still need to cool down, however. And they do this partly by radiating heat from the shaded underside of their bodies, where the coat is thin. They also sweat to keep cool. The pores of the skin give off moisture, which evaporates in the air, taking heat from the skin, and so cooling it.

The reason these animals, and indeed all mammals, must keep cool is that they are warm-blooded, and their body can only work within quite a narrow temperature range. A rise of just a few degrees in a human being, for example, can be life-threatening.

But some desert animals, including the camel, are able to let their body temperature rise by as much as 11°F without any danger. This reduces the need for them to sweat so much, which in turn reduces the loss of precious body water.

SAVANNAH

A group of giraffes stretch their long necks to feed on the leaves at the top of one of the trees that are scattered over the African savannah. It is the middle of the dry season and the grasses have already shriveled up. Many zebras, wildebeest, and other grazing animals are dying through lack of food. The giraffes, however, still look healthy because they can get at food the other animals cannot reach.

The vast, grass-covered plains that lie on either side of the tropical rain forests in central Africa support not only giraffes and zebras but many other large animals too. These plains form the largest area of the biome known as the savannah.

There are smaller areas in other parts of the world. In southern Africa they are called the veld. In South America the large region of tropical grassland south of the rain forests is called the llanos. Smaller savannah regions are found in Madagascar and southern Australia.

WET AND DRY

The savannah has quite a plentiful rainfall, up to 60in in a few parts. But the rain falls only for part of the year, during the wet season. During the rest of the year – the dry season – it does not rain at all. The length of the dry season varies from place to place and from year to year, but is often 6 months or more. The lack of water, coupled with high temperatures (up to 95°F) makes the dry season a testing time for both plant and animal life.

▲A zebra tries to escape from a hungry cheetah, but it is hopeless. The cheetah is much too fast for it, being able to reach speeds of over 60mph.

The typical vegetation of the savannah is grassland with scattered clumps of trees. There is a mix of tall and short grasses. Where conditions are favorable, tall grasses like the African Napier grass may even grow several feet high. The trees of the savannah are usually not very tall and have small

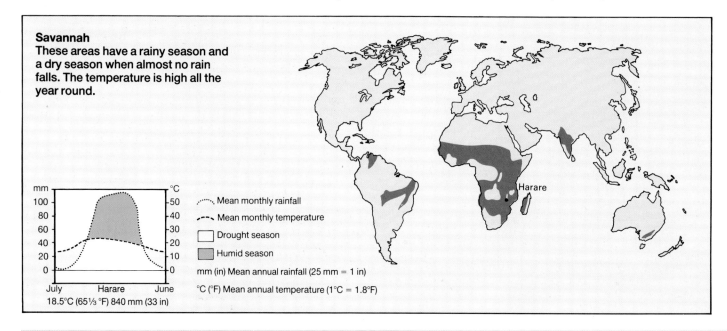

Savannah
These areas have a rainy season and a dry season when almost no rain falls. The temperature is high all the year round.

mm .... Mean monthly rainfall

--- Mean monthly temperature

☐ Drought season

▨ Humid season

mm (in) Mean annual rainfall (25 mm = 1 in)

°C (°F) Mean annual temperature (1°C = 1.8°F)

July Harare June
18.5°C (65⅓ °F) 840 mm (33 in)

Harare

◄A lioness rests amid the luxuriant vegetation of the African savannah. This is the wet season, when the grass is lush and flowers bloom in abundance. The grass-eating animals thrive and roam far from their waterholes. Lions find it easier hunting in such dense cover.

▼A herd of African elephants makes its way noisily through the tall savannah vegetation. The landscape is covered in flowers, for again this is the wet season. In a few weeks, however, the rains will cease and so will plant growth. The vegetation will soon turn brown in the relentless Sun and the drought. The animals will drift back to the waterholes, which will become the hub of their life until the next rains.

leaves and thorny branches. The acacias of Africa are typical. The most remarkable African tree, however, is the baobab, or bottle tree. It has spindly branches but a thick trunk, in which it stores water to live on during the dry season. In Australia the typical savannah tree is the eucalyptus, which is well-suited to surviving the fires that regularly sweep over the grassland regions.

GRAZERS AND BROWSERS

The African savannah supports vast herds of many species of herbivores, or grazing animals. Prominent among these are zebra, gnu, wildebeest, gazelle, impala and other antelopes.

These animals do not all feed in the same way. If they did, the grasslands could not support them.

Some species, such as giraffes, prefer to eat specific plants. Others feed in succession on the grass. The Plains zebra, for example, grazes on tall grass. The Brindled gnu prefers shorter grass, and Thomson's gazelle grazes on the short grass left behind by the zebras and gnu. So herds of these three species tend to follow each other across the savannah.

The biggest herds are often to be seen during the dry season, when animals head for new feeding grounds. Other animals, including the Common eland, browse on the leaves

of shrubs and trees in addition to grazing. Elephants feed on a wide range of vegetation, and have a major effect on the landscape by uprooting trees and shrubs.

Any vegetation that the grazers leave provides food for the detritivores – those creatures that live on detritus, or discarded material. The most important are the termites.

▼A flock of Marabou storks roosts as the Sun goes down on the African savannah. These birds are scavengers and feed on carrion. They nest in the dry season when prey is concentrated near the waterholes, and they can find plenty of food for their young.

▼Various species of South American savannah animals The Burrowing owl (*Athene cunicularia*) **(1)** of treeless grassland. The Southern tamandua (*Tamandua tetradactyla*) **(2)** and the Great-banded armadillo (*Dasypus novemcinctus*) **(3)**.

They build nest mounds which are several feet high and form a distinctive feature of the savannah.

PREDATORS AND SCAVENGERS

The wide variety of large herbivores provides rich pickings for many predators, particularly in Africa. Foremost among them is the lion, a majestic creature, well named "king of the beasts." Lions usually need to stalk their prey and surprise it, because they do not have the speed to outrun it. The cheetah, however, can outrun any other animal.

Other major carnivores include the African wild dog, the jackal and the hyena. The wild dogs hunt in packs and can bring down prey as large as zebras. Jackals take smaller prey and also feed on carrion. Hyenas are hunters and scavengers, and they often chase lions away from a kill.

▼Animal dung provides food for the dung beetles. Here two females are feeding. Dung beetles also collect balls of dung and roll them into their burrows. They lay their eggs on these balls, which provides nourishment for the larvae when they hatch.

PRAIRIE

A hungry coyote slinks through the prairie grass, hoping to sneak up on one of the prairie dogs sitting near the entrance to a burrow. Closer and closer the coyote creeps and still its intended victim hasn't seen it. But just as it is about to pounce, one of the prairie dog's neighbors spots it and gives out a warning call. The prairie dog just has time to dive into its burrow. It will remain there until it hears the "all-clear" call.

The prairie dog and its predator, the coyote, are both natives of the American prairies, which form part of the biome of temperate grasslands. These grasslands occupy vast areas of North America and Eurasia. In Asia they are known as the steppes. A much smaller region of temperate grassland, known as the pampas, is found in South America, mainly in Argentina.

Lying in the middle of the continents, these grasslands have a fairly dry climate, with hot summers and cold winters. In the eastern steppes, for example, the daytime temperature averages up to 77°F in the summer while dropping below −5°F in the winter. Rainfall averages only about 2½in every year.

In the western steppes the temperature difference between summer and winter is much less, and up to 16in of rain falls. This climate provides ideal growing conditions for grass, and also for all the cultivated grasses we know as cereals – wheat, oats and barley. That is why vast regions of the western steppes are given over to agricultural use. The same is true of the North American prairies and the Argentinian pampas.

BISON AND DEER

Farming, therefore, has made the temperate grasslands very much a disturbed habitat for the native wildlife. Naturally, the main native animals of the region are grazers – herbivores. In the past the American prairies were dominated by bison, or American buffalo, which could be numbered in millions. But wholesale slaughter by settlers nearly wiped out the species. It was a very similar story with the

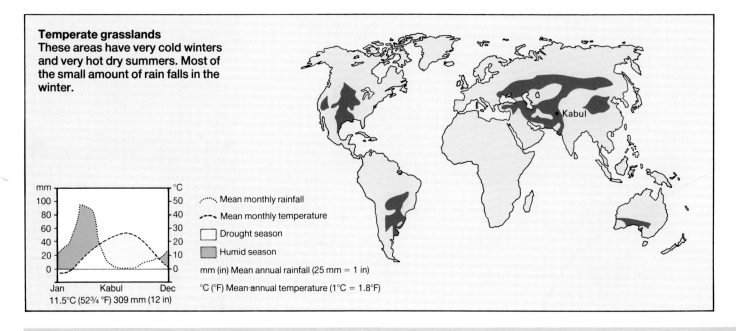

Temperate grasslands
These areas have very cold winters and very hot dry summers. Most of the small amount of rain falls in the winter.

.... Mean monthly rainfall

- - - Mean monthly temperature

☐ Drought season

▨ Humid season

mm (in) Mean annual rainfall (25 mm = 1 in)

°C (°F) Mean annual temperature (1°C = 1.8°F)

Jan — Kabul — Dec
11.5°C (52¾ °F) 309 mm (12 in)

◄A herd of American bison or buffalo grazes on the grasslands of North Dakota. Millions of these large herbivores once roamed the American prairies but buffalo hunting in the 1800s reduced their numbers to just a few hundred. Under protection, they have again increased to over 40,000.

►A group of Roe deer grazing. It is early summer and the deer's gray winter coat has changed to fox-red for the summer.

▼A herd of pronghorns on the prairie in Wyoming, USA. Like the buffalo, the pronghorn was almost hunted to extinction in the 1800s. But under protection its population has increased to several hundred thousand.

European bison, or wisent, which lived on the Eurasian steppes. Protection has helped both species survive.

The other large herbivore of the prairies is the pronghorn, a deer-like animal with distinctive prongs on its horns. On the Eurasian steppes Red and Roe deer occupy this niche.

On the pampas there are no really large herbivores. The largest are the Pampas deer and the guanaco, a relative of the camel. The large flightless birds known as rheas also feed mainly on the grass.

RODENT LIFE
The main animals of the pampas are burrowing rodents. They include the Plains viscacha, the males of which weigh up to 18lb. Other rodents include the mara and the tuco-tuco.

On the prairies, ground squirrels and prairie dogs occupy a similar niche. The prairie dog is a member of the squirrel family and is a very social animal. Large numbers of prairie dogs live together in a social group called a coterie. The animals dig an extensive network of tunnels and chambers for shelter and for raising their young.

Often numerous coteries group together and form a "town" covering as much as 160 acres. On the steppes the souslik has a similar life-style. Among the other rodents that live there is the Common hamster, familiar to pet lovers.

THE PREDATORS
In all three main temperate grassland regions there are similar predators. The largest are dog-like animals, such as wolves and foxes. They feed mainly on rodents and nesting birds. Other predators include weasels, badgers and birds of prey. On the prairies the American badger is a more determined hunter than the Eurasian species, actively digging out ground squirrels and even taking rattlesnakes.

▶ ▼ Prairie dogs pictured on the entrance mound of their burrow. These rodents dig out tunnels and chambers underground for shelter and for raising their young. Other animals, for instance badgers, may invade these tunnels in search of prey or, like the Burrowing owl, take them over after the prairie dogs have left.

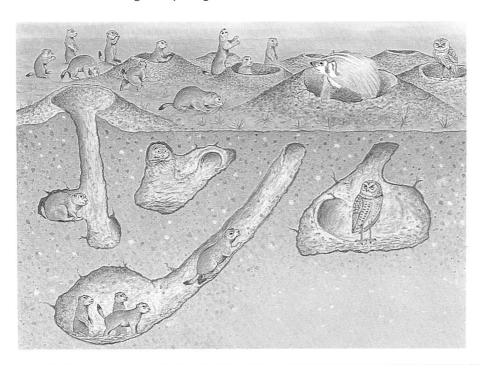

TUNDRA

Driven by instinct, a group of lemmings is migrating. They are moving along a track, which narrows as it winds along the river bank. Another group joins them from another track. Suddenly both groups panic and rush blindly ahead. The track is not wide enough to take all the frantic horde. First one or two, then many get pushed over the edge of the bank into the river. Soon the water is a seething mass of panicking animals trying to swim and fighting for breath. Some make it safely to the river bank, but many drown.

Lemmings survive and multiply in one of the harshest climates on Earth – in part of the region in the extreme north of North America, Europe and Asia called the tundra. In winter the temperature in places may drop to −60°F, and the Sun may not shine for days on end. Frost may occur even in summer. Much of the ground is permanently frozen – it is known as permafrost – and less rain falls here than in some of the deserts.

Yet despite the severity of the climate, plants and animals live in this biome which extends north from the boreal forest regions in Europe, North America and Asia.

Most of the tundra lies around the Arctic Ocean and inside the Arctic Circle (latitude 66½°), but in North America it extends farther south. There is a smaller area of tundra in northern Europe than expected because the land there is warmed by the Gulf Stream ocean current.

In the Southern hemisphere there are only scattered regions of tundra, for example, on the Falkland Islands. Most of the great mass of Antarctica itself is covered in snow and ice the whole year round.

A tundra-type region also exists near the top of high mountains, where the climate is similar. This type of biome is often called alpine tundra.

TUNDRA LANDSCAPE

Perennials – plants that come up year after year – are the commonest plants on the tundra. Among the most successful are the many saxifrage and crowberry species, which have a compact, low-growing form to combat the cold winds.

Other plants include sedge and cotton-grass. A few shrubs and trees are found in some regions, mainly willows and birch. But these grow as dwarfs, only 3ft or so high.

Most tundra plants have a very rapid life cycle in order to cope with the limited growing season, which may be as short as just 2 months. They flower a few days after the snows have melted and quickly produce seeds just a month or so later.

As the summer snows melt and the upper soil thaws, much of the ground becomes boggy. This is because the lower soil – the permafrost – remains frozen and so prevents the surface water from draining away.

RESIDENTS AND MIGRANTS

The summer growth of vegetation on the tundra attracts a number of large herbivores, or plant-eaters. From the boreal forests come the caribou and reindeer. They join the herds of Musk oxen, which live on the tundra winter and summer. They can survive the freezing cold winter because of their exceptionally thick coat and thick layers of body fat. Musk oxen often huddle together for warmth and for protection against predators.

Among the other permanent residents of the tundra are the lemmings. Lemming numbers vary wildly from year to year. They are very rapid breeders, the females being able to give birth to their first litter of young when less than 40 days old. Every 4

▲ In the short summer, birds flock to the Arctic tundra to breed and feed on the vegetation and the plentiful insect life. These are White-fronted geese.

▲ The Musk ox is a large beast, weighing up to 770lb in the wild. Its thick, shaggy coat protects it from the bitter cold of the Arctic winters.

▶ The Norway lemming, which lives in northern Scandinavia and north-west Russia. It has specially adapted claws for digging in the snow for food.

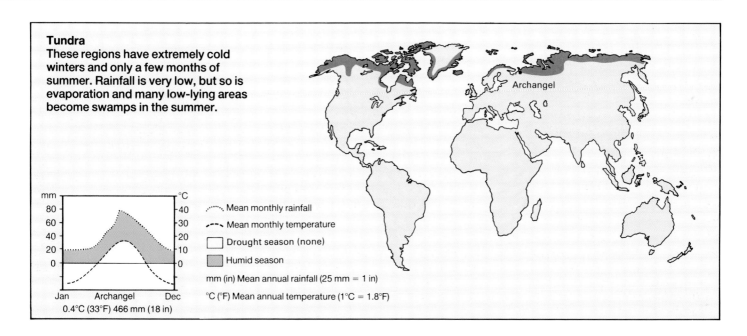

Tundra
These regions have extremely cold winters and only a few months of summer. Rainfall is very low, but so is evaporation and many low-lying areas become swamps in the summer.

Archangel

.... Mean monthly rainfall

- - - - Mean monthly temperature

☐ Drought season (none)

▨ Humid season

mm (in) Mean annual rainfall (25 mm = 1 in)

°C (°F) Mean annual temperature (1°C = 1.8°F)

Archangel
0.4°C (33°F) 466 mm (18 in)

years or so lemming populations become so high that they have to migrate to new feeding grounds. Mass migrations occur involving thousands of animals, often in a state of panic.

THE PREDATORS
The lemming and another tundra resident, the Arctic hare, are prey for a number of predators. Among them are the stoat and Arctic fox. The Arctic fox, Arctic hare and stoat all have a brownish coat in summer, which turns white in winter to camouflage the animals in the snow.

Other predators, such as wolves, wolverines and Brown bears, follow the caribou and reindeer out of the forests onto the tundra in summer, and prey particularly on their young as well as on smaller mammals. One of the most formidable predators of the north, however, is the Polar bear. It is not found on the tundra itself, but usually on ice floes. It feeds mainly on seals, especially Ringed seals. Wolves and Arctic foxes often follow Polar bears to feed on any leftovers.

BIRD LIFE
Several birds of prey attack small mammals, such as the lemmings and Arctic hare. The main resident bird of prey is the Snowy owl, joined in the summer by buzzards, jaegers (skuas) and falcons.

►An Arctic fox in its white winter coat. This remarkable animal does not start shivering until the temperature drops to below −60°F.

These last two species are attracted by birds like the Arctic warbler, which have migrated to the tundra to feed on the plentiful insect life that thrives in the boggy tundra region. The insects include blackflies and mosquitoes, which attack any warm-blooded animal for a blood meal, making their life a misery. To escape these swarms of irritating insects, caribou and reindeer move away from the low-lying swamps onto higher, drier ground.

Vast flocks of geese also migrate to the tundra in summer to breed. They include the Graylag, White-fronted, Snow and Canada geese. As the summer draws to a close, they wing their way back south to the British Isles, the Mediterranean region or the southern United States.

FROM POLE TO POLE

The greatest migration, however, is made by the Arctic tern. It nests in the tundra in the Arctic summer, then flies more than 3,750mi to the Antarctic for its summer before returning once again to the Arctic.

Both the Arctic and Antarctic are in continuous daylight during their summers, so this bird probably enjoys more daylight and less darkness than any other species on Earth. Its twice yearly journey from pole to pole is the longest migration route of any animal.

◄On the Arctic tundra Polar bears are the top carnivores. They feed mainly on seals and walruses, and occasionaly on smaller mammals and birds.

►A Gray wolf, the largest member of the dog family. This is a youngster, which has left the pack in which it was born to seek a mate and set up its own territory.

MOUNTAINS

It is late fall in the Swiss Alps, and the days are drawing in. A plump animal with thick grayish-brown fur is waddling towards its burrow beneath a boulder, carrying dried grass in its mouth. It is an Alpine marmot. It disappears underground to a chamber and spreads out the grass. Later other members of the family group join in. In a few days the chamber has become a cosy den. As the cold sets in, the family retire to the burrow. The last animal in plugs the entrance hole with grass and soil. The time has come for the long winter sleep.

The Alps, the highest mountains in Europe, are just one of the world's great mountain ranges. All mountains have a different kind of climate from that of the land around them. This is mainly because the temperature falls steadily with increasing height, or altitude. On average the temperature drops about one degree for every 300ft rise above sea level.

▶ **Typical animal and plant life on Mount Kenya, East Africa** All around the mountain is savannah grassland and scattered trees. Higher up is a thick rain forest of tree ferns and other tropical trees. Then comes a mixed forest, including a region of bamboo before the trees give way to low shrubby vegetation, including the extraordinary giant groundsel. Higher still comes short sparse grassland, which ends at the snowline.

The change in temperature that occurs with increasing altitude is similar to the change in temperature that occurs over increasing latitudes, or increasing distances from the equator.

The temperature change with latitude gives rise to the world climatic zones – equatorial, temperate, and so on. The temperature change with altitude produces the equivalent climatic zones going up a mountain. Each will favor certain types of plants and animals. In other words, a mountain creates its own set of biomes.

UP THE HIMALAYAS

The change in climate with altitude is well illustrated by the Himalayan mountain range. These mountains are located just outside the tropics, and their lower slopes, or foothills, are covered with luxuriant subtropical forest. Above about 4,600ft the climate becomes temperate and leads to deciduous forest of oak and rhododendron. From about 8,000ft conifers such as deodar, pine and fir take over. This zone is equivalent to the boreal forest region of the high northern latitudes.

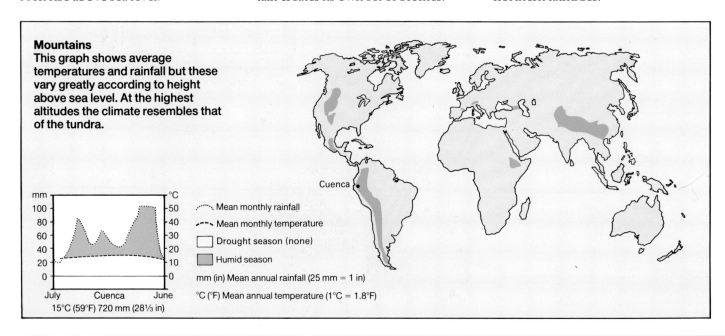

Mountains
This graph shows average temperatures and rainfall but these vary greatly according to height above sea level. At the highest altitudes the climate resembles that of the tundra.

······· Mean monthly rainfall

------ Mean monthly temperature

☐ Drought season (none)

▨ Humid season

mm (in) Mean annual rainfall (25 mm = 1 in)

°C (°F) Mean annual temperature (1°C = 1.8°F)

Cuenca

July   Cuenca   June
15°C (59°F) 720 mm (28⅓ in)

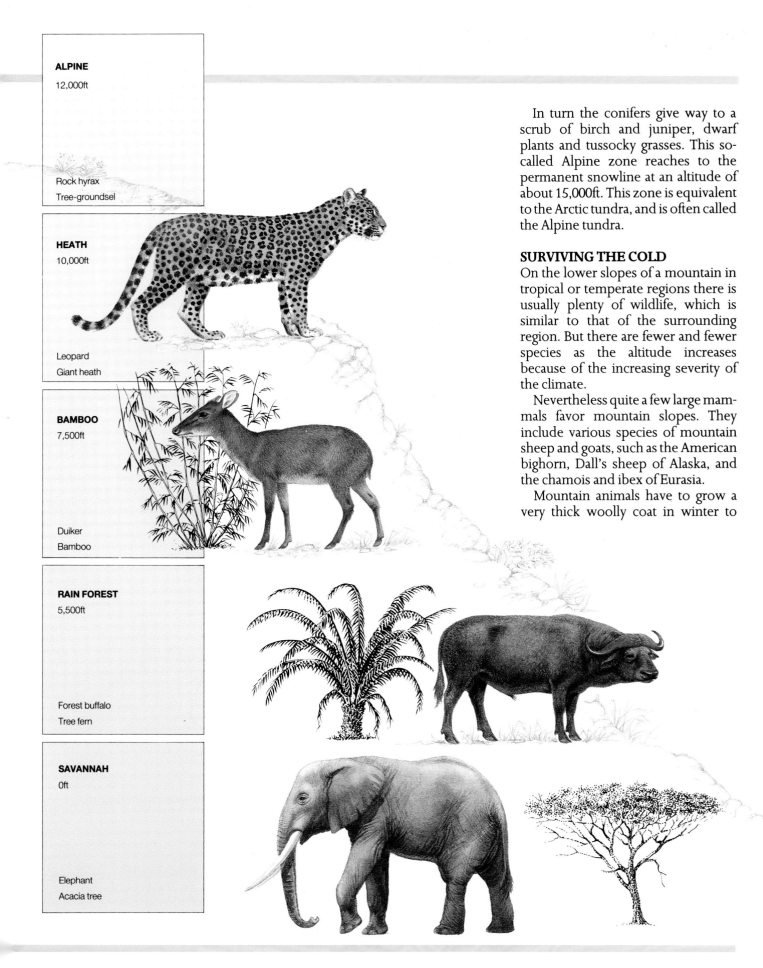

ALPINE

12,000ft

Rock hyrax
Tree-groundsel

HEATH

10,000ft

Leopard
Giant heath

BAMBOO

7,500ft

Duiker
Bamboo

RAIN FOREST

5,500ft

Forest buffalo
Tree fern

SAVANNAH

0ft

Elephant
Acacia tree

In turn the conifers give way to a scrub of birch and juniper, dwarf plants and tussocky grasses. This so-called Alpine zone reaches to the permanent snowline at an altitude of about 15,000ft. This zone is equivalent to the Arctic tundra, and is often called the Alpine tundra.

SURVIVING THE COLD

On the lower slopes of a mountain in tropical or temperate regions there is usually plenty of wildlife, which is similar to that of the surrounding region. But there are fewer and fewer species as the altitude increases because of the increasing severity of the climate.

Nevertheless quite a few large mammals favor mountain slopes. They include various species of mountain sheep and goats, such as the American bighorn, Dall's sheep of Alaska, and the chamois and ibex of Eurasia.

Mountain animals have to grow a very thick woolly coat in winter to keep out the cold. The chinchilla, a rodent, and the camel-like alpaca, both of the Andes, have exceptionally warm coats. So has the Angora goat of Central Asia. All three species are farmed for their coats, the Angora yielding the fiber called mohair.

There are only a few large predators in high mountain regions because of the limited supply of prey. The Rocky Mountains of North America are the haunt of the puma, also called the Mountain lion. In the Himalayas and the highlands of eastern China lives the beautiful Snow leopard, which preys mainly on ibex. Wolves are also found in some mountain regions where they hunt sheep.

▼The vicuña in its high mountain habitat. This camel-like animal lives in the Andes Mountains of South America.

►A group of ibex, which live at high altitudes in Europe and Asia. Ibex have massive horns, up to 4½ft in length.

MIGRATE OR HIBERNATE

Many of the larger mammals and the beasts that prey on them avoid the worst cold of winter by migrating down the mountains into the shelter and higher temperature of the forests.

Many small mammals, on the other hand, hibernate. They include ground squirrels and marmots, which may

▼A puma, also called a Mountain lion, pictured in the mixed forest of the Rocky Mountains in the United States.

spend half the year asleep. During the summer, these animals gorge themselves to build up a thick layer of fat, which sustains them through the winter with little or no food.

HIGH WINDS

The high Alpine peaks are buffeted by strong winds much of the time, and birds are few and far between. Only strong fliers can cope with them. They include in the high Andes the condor and in Eurasia the lammergeier. The

lammergeier is a scavenger, which feeds on carrion. It sometimes drops bones from a great height to crack them open and get at the marrow they contain. A common bird at lower altitudes is the ptarmigan, which has a white winter plumage for camouflage.

The high winds also discourage winged insects. Most of the native species, such as the grylloblattids of the Rocky Mountains, are wingless. They feed on insects the wind has blown up from lower altitudes.

RIVERS

The water is tumbling swiftly down the mountainside, rushing between the stones that litter the stream bed. On one of these stones is a plump, wren-like bird, which constantly bobs up and down. It is a dipper. It hops down into the water and, walking on the bottom, disappears under the surface. With head down, it walks upstream, probing for insect larvae and crustaceans among the stones. Nearly half a minute later it surfaces, and with larvae wriggling in its bill, it flies back to its nest to feed its five hungry hatchlings.

Although nearly three-quarters of the Earth's surface is covered with water, the dipper's rushing freshwater streams form only a tiny fraction of it. Most of the Earth's water fills the great oceans and is salty. Only about 3 percent is fresh water, and only about half of this is liquid water flowing in rivers and streams, or trapped in

▲ The American dipper lives beside swift-flowing streams from Alaska to Central America. It builds a dome-shaped nest of moss, lined with grass and leaves, usually above running water.

◄ Two male Mute swans fighting, because one has intruded into the other's territory. The fight is furious, with much hissing and wing flapping. Almost always the resident wins such a bout.

► A water spider with its "diving bell." It spins this structure to trap air to breathe so that it can remain underwater for long periods.

lakes and ponds. The rest is frozen as ice or snow in the Arctic and Antarctic and on high mountains.

Fresh and salty water provide quite different conditions for living things and, as a result, contain quite different plant and animal life. Only a few species spend their lives, or part of their lives, in both fresh and saline (salty) waters. They include fish such as the salmon and the freshwater eel.

FEEDING THE FISH

As with other habitats, every body of water has a food chain. At the bottom of the chain is plant material.

▼A pair of damselflies mating on a reed. The blue male holds the head of the female in special pincers, while she receives sperm from his body. Then she will lay eggs from her egg-laying tube, or ovipositor. She uses this to pierce the reed and lay eggs inside it.

This may come from the outside in the form of dead leaves. Or it may come from simple plants that grow in the water and make their food by photosynthesis. These plants include single-celled plants such as algae.

In turn simple plants are "grazed" by tiny creatures called zooplankton and by crustaceans, creatures like *Cyclops*. Then higher creatures such as fish eat the zooplankton and crustaceans, and may in turn be eaten by bigger fish.

Water life is not as plentiful in rivers as in the still waters of ponds and lakes. In rivers the current, which is swiftest in the higher upper reaches of a river, sweeps the food supplies downstream.

SUCKERS AND BARBELS

The main creatures that live in the swift-flowing water are invertebrates that keep to the river bed – insect

larvae, leeches, and molluscs such as water snails. The larvae of mayflies and caddisflies are specially adapted for life in fast currents. They have little suckers or hooks on their bodies to anchor themselves to the stones.

As the river flows down into the lowlands, it becomes deeper, wider and slower. As it becomes slower, more plant material and dirt particles can settle out, producing a muddy sediment on the bottom. Also, as the river slows, more vegetation grows along its banks providing food and shelter for a wide variety of wildlife.

The sediment on the river bed becomes the home of burrowing creatures, including various worms, and molluscs such as clams and mussels. Insect larvae still abound in the upper layers of sediment, as do crustaceans like the freshwater shrimp. The typical fish of the lower

reaches of the river is the barbel, named for the barbels, or fleshy feelers, on its lower jaw.

DIPPERS, DIVERS AND BATHERS
Among the birds that live around the fast-flowing upper reaches are the dipper and, in the Andes Mountains, the well-named Torrent duck. This duck is well adapted for its habitat, having a streamlined shape and sharp claws for gripping slippery boulders. Many other species of ducks and swans are to be found on the lower reaches of most rivers. Moorhens and coots are also very common, as are kingfishers and herons.

The water is not the natural home of many mammals, but several do spend much of their time in it. They include the water vole, which lives in the river bank, and the otter, one of the finest swimmers of the animal world. In rivers in tropical Africa hippopotamuses ("river horses") spend the day in the river to keep cool.

Manatees are truly aquatic mammals. They live in estuaries and rivers in South America and the southern United States. River dolphins are also aquatic. They live in the estuaries of great rivers such as the Ganges and Indus in India and the Amazon in South America.

▼Manatees playing in the Crystal River, Florida. They have a streamlined body, rather like a seal's, but are stockier and have a blunt head. Unlike seals too they are herbivores, feeding on aquatic plants such as water weeds and seagrass.

▶A Brown trout swims over a gravel river bed and among water plants in Hampshire, England. Some Brown trout migrate to the sea to feed (and are also called Sea or Salmon trout), others spend their lives in lakes.

PONDS AND LAKES

The six fluffy black moorhen chicks have recently hatched. With their parents, they are searching for food among the lily pads and weeds that grow in the lake. Some are walking on the leaves, others are swimming in the water. All is calm. Suddenly there is an ominous swirl in the water and one chick disappears. The others scatter in panic. Underwater a pike has the chick clamped in its razor-sharp teeth. The chick struggles, but in vain. There is no escape from such a vicious predator.

The still waters of ponds and lakes provide a favorable environment not only for waterfowl, but for a great variety of plant and animal life. Free-floating microscopic plants such as algae provide the main source of food.

In a river this resource is carried away by the current, but in still water it remains and builds up. The microscopic plants multiply in the water as they undergo photosynthesis. Such plants, known as phytoplankton, undergo an explosion of growth in the spring, when the waters are said to "bloom." Dead leaves and other organic debris, or detritus, are another food resource that builds up on the bottom as a muddy sediment.

TOO MUCH OF A GOOD THING

The abundance and variety of life in a lake depend to a large extent on the nature of the local soils and rocks. The most productive lakes are rich in dissolved mineral matter such as calcium, together with nitrogen and other elements essential for plant growth. Molluscs, worms, flatworms and crustaceans thrive in such water.

Because of the abundance of the plant life, especially plankton, in such lakes, the water is usually green and opaque. And there is usually lush growth of vegetation, such as reeds and water lilies at the water's edge. Such lakes are termed eutrophic.

In many ponds and lakes in farming areas, serious problems are being caused by the run-off of nitrates from the fertilizers applied to the surrounding land. This leads to eutrophication – very rapid plant growth and the build-up of thick layers of dead material on the bottom. As this decomposes, it takes much of the oxygen from the water, which reduces the numbers of fish and other animals that depend on dissolved oxygen to breathe.

▲Some animals that live in and around a European lake In the swampy area of the reed bed are a Sedge warbler (*Acrocephalus schoenobaenus*) (1) and European water vole (*Arvicola terrestris*) (2). In the shallows among aquatic plants are the Common frog (*Rana temporaria*) (3), the Gray moorhen (*Gallinula chloropus*) (4) and the mayfly and its larva (5). In deeper water, which has submerged plants rooted at the bottom, are the Water boatman (*Notoneta glauca*) (6), Great pond snail (*Limnea stagnalis*) (7), Tufted duck (*Aythya fuligula*) (8), flatworm (*Planaria* species) (9) and perch (*Perca fluviatilis*) (10).

Lakes in regions of acid-rich soils, such as peat moors, are quite different. They have brown water due to the presence of acids and suspended plant material. Their life is limited to a few insect species. The clear water of lakes in hard-rock areas are rich in oxygen, but lacking in plankton. And life is limited there too.

▶ A Roseate spoonbill probes into the muddy bottom of a lake searching for creatures to eat. Because the water is muddy, it finds its prey by touch. It probes with its bill open, and snaps it shut if it feels something moving.

▲ Microscopic algae like this are found in lakes and ponds. They are the main food source for animal life, being at the bottom of the food chain.

▼ Among the animals that graze on pond plants is the Great pond snail. This one has just laid a "rope" of eggs, which are now attached to its shell.

LAKE ANIMALS

At the lowest level of animal life in ponds and lakes are the tiny creatures that feed on the phytoplankton in the water. They are called zooplankton. They include the single-celled microscopic protozoans; rotifers, which can just about be seen with the naked eye; and crustaceans such as *Daphnia*, less than ¼in long.

The zooplankton, in turn, are a food source for other animals. The larvae of many insects including mosquito, caddisfly and mayfly, feed on them. So do some fish, including the stickleback. Other fish, and amphibians such as frogs and newts, feed on the larvae. Then these animals may be eaten by higher predators, including top carnivore fish such as pike, and waterbirds such as kingfishers and herons.

The fish and other free-swimming creatures of the lakes make up what is called the nekton. This contrasts with the plankton, made up of organisms that merely float.

ON THE BOTTOM

The lake bottom, where organic matter has settled out, is also usually a rich source of food. This detritus provides nourishment for molluscs such as water snails, various worms, and crustaceans – creatures with jointed limbs and shells, such as shrimps. Bacteria also break down the detritus, and are a further food source.

The lake plants themselves are also grazed by fish, ducks, larvae and molluscs. The larger plants are not so useful as food, but provide shelter from predators. They also play a vital role in the life-cycle of species. Insects like dragonflies and damselflies use plant stems to enter the water and deposit their eggs. Later the stems provide the means for the insect larvae or nymphs to leave the water. They eventually metamorphose into adults, ready to take flight.

Insects and the other animals that live at the bottom are called benthos.

Food web in a temperate lake

- First trophic level (primary producers)
- Second trophic level (herbivores)
- Third trophic level
- Fourth trophic level
- Fifth trophic level
- Sixth trophic level

Frog/tadpole

Duck

Leech

Caddisfly larva

Bitterling

▲ **The food web in a lake in temperate regions** A food web links organisms by their feeding habits. Feeding takes place at various levels, called trophic levels. Plants are the primary producers and form the first trophic level. Creatures that eat plants form the second level; animals that eat those creatures form the third trophic level; and so on. In the picture the animals at the various trophic levels are drawn with a coded color background. The eating habits of each animal are shown by the arrows.

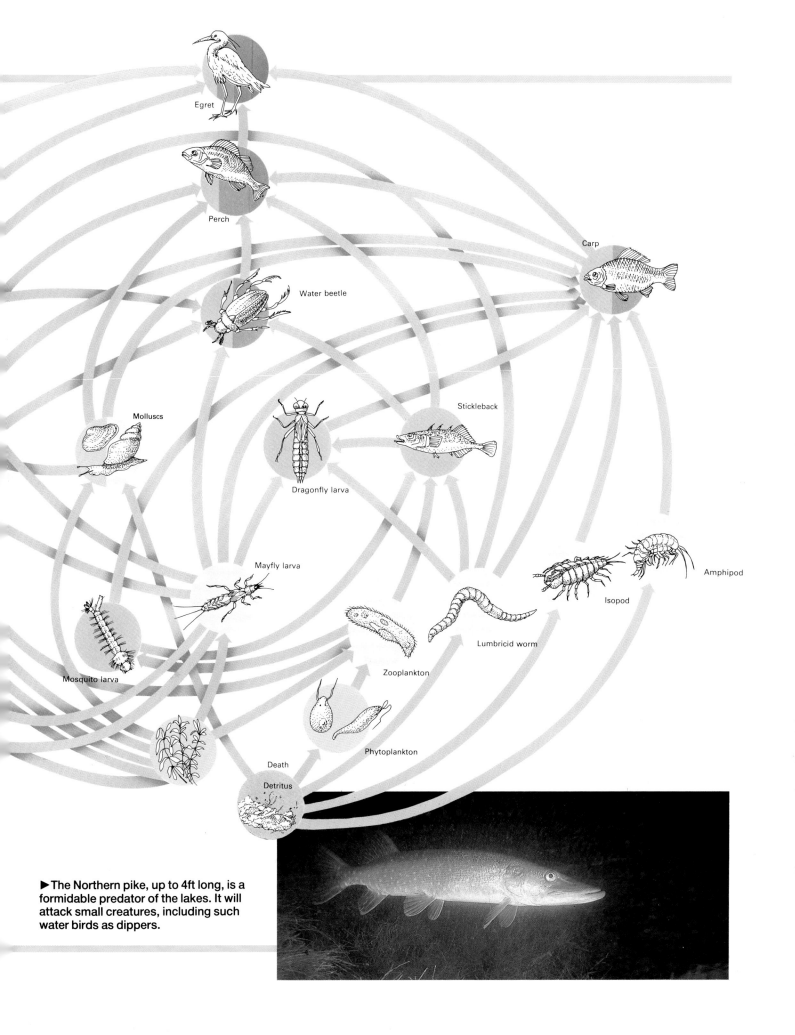

Egret

Perch

Carp

Water beetle

Molluscs

Stickleback

Dragonfly larva

Mayfly larva

Amphipod

Isopod

Lumbricid worm

Mosquito larva

Zooplankton

Death

Phytoplankton

Detritus

►The Northern pike, up to 4ft long, is a formidable predator of the lakes. It will attack small creatures, including such water birds as dippers.

FRESHWATER WETLAND

A group of capybaras, the world's largest rodents, are resting at the water's edge in a South American swamp. Some are dozing, but a few are still alert. One spots a caiman, a kind of alligator, swimming nearby and lets out a loud bark. In a flash the others stand alert ready to flee if there is immediate danger. This time there isn't, for the caiman has recently eaten its fill.

Not only in South America but throughout the world there are low-lying regions where fresh water stays on the surface instead of draining away into the ground or into rivers. These areas are called swamps or marshes, or, generally, wetlands. The term swamp refers to a wetland of trees; and a marsh to a wetland of grasses and other low plants.

Vast swamp and marsh areas are found on the flood plains and deltas (river mouths with many channels) of many of the world's great rivers; for example, the Amazon in South America, the Nile in Egypt and the Mekong in Vietnam. In Europe the Coto de Doñana of south-western Spain and the Carmargue region of the Rhône delta in France are notable marsh areas.

In the United States there is a vast swamp and marsh region in North Carolina and Virginia, called the Great Dismal Swamp. In Florida are the great Cypress Swamp and the Everglades. The Everglades region is like a slow-moving river about 6in deep. It covers an area of 3,800 sq mi.

REEDS AND GRASSES

The main plants that grow in swamps and marshes are grasses and reeds, or rushes. Bulrushes, also called cattails and reedmaces, are found in many

▲ Toads are common in freshwater wetlands. They spend more time on land than frogs, only returning to the water each spring to spawn. Their eggs are laid in long strings, unlike frogspawn.

▲An American alligator moves through the Everglades, looking for turtles, birds and small mammals to eat. Fully grown adults are up to 18ft in length.

◀A group of lechwe chasing through the water of the flood plain in Botswana. Lechwe usually graze in shallow water, but occasionally venture shoulder-high in search of food.

parts of the world. So are various species of the common water reed which grow up to about 8ft tall. The reed-like papyrus is common in tropical and subtropical Africa, where it grows up to 20ft tall.

MAMMALS IN MUDDY WATERS
In general, wetlands are not a suitable habitat for large mammals because of the difficulty of moving around. The hippopotamus of the African papyrus swamps is an exception. It can weigh up to 2½ tons and spends most of its time wallowing in the muddy waters. Its feces, or dung, adds many nutrients to the water, so helping the growth of plant life.

Among other mammals of these swamps are the sitatunga and lechwe. The hooves of these antelopes are specially adapted for their life in the swamps. They splay out widely to distribute the animal's weight and prevent it sinking in the mud.

The swamps of North America are inhabited by smaller mammals, especially the muskrat, a large water vole. It eats vegetation as well as molluscs and crustaceans. An interesting animal is the Swamp rabbit, which does not jump like most other rabbits, but is a good swimmer. These two mammals are preyed on by the American mink, which is an excellent swimmer and also eats fish, frogs, snakes and waterbirds.

AMPHIBIANS AND ALLIGATORS
Marshlands are rich in amphibians and reptiles. The most familiar amphibians are frogs and toads, of which in

all there are over three thousand species. Most of them are found in wetlands, as are species of the other amphibians, the newts and salamanders. Amphibians feed on insects, molluscs, spiders and other invertebrates. They are preyed upon by many birds, reptiles and mammals.

The largest reptiles are the alligators and crocodiles. Of these reptiles, the American alligator of the southern United States is found in the largest numbers. Elsewhere most alligator and crocodile species are threatened by overhunting and habitat destruction. They are formidable predators, able to kill animals as big as cattle.

Snakes are also found widely. They move easily through the swampy vegetation and many are good swimmers. They feed on lizards, amphibians, nestlings and small mammals.

BIRD LIFE

Many open wetlands support a rich variety of bird life. The Everglades in Florida is the home of both tropical and temperate species. These include flamingos, Roseate spoonbills, Bald eagles and ospreys.

The many different bird species are each suited for a particular feeding niche. Long-legged birds like the flamingo are able to feed on fauna living in deep water. Shorter-legged species feed in the shallows. Some stab at prey with sharp bills; others sift the muddy water with their spoon-shaped bills.

▶**Some birds of the Coto de Doñana wetlands in Spain** Among the waterfowl are the Marbled teal (*Marmaronetta angustirostris*) **(1)** and the Ruddy shelduck (*Tadorna ferruginea*) **(2)**. The Marsh harrier (*Circus aeruginosus*) **(3)** is the main bird of prey. The Whiskered tern (*Chlidonias hybrida*) **(4)** and Greater flamingo (*Phoenicopterus ruber*) **(5)** nest in number. The Cattle egret (*Bubulcus ibis*) **(6)** is a small heron. The feet of the Purple swamp hen (*Porphyrio porphyrio*) **(7)** are specially adapted for walking on floating vegetation. The Black-crowned night heron (*Nycticorax nycticorax*) **(8)** feeds at night but also by day. The Great reed warbler (*Acrocephalus arundinaceus*) **(9)** nests among the reeds.

BOGS

Bogs are wetlands with organic or peaty soil. They occur in northern temperate regions where the decomposition of plant material takes place very slowly. They also occur in the tundra regions of North America, Europe and Asia. The main vegetation is sphagnum moss. The moss absorbs nearly all the nourishment from the water and makes it acid.

Compared with the other wetlands, the bogs support little animal life. The water is too acid and lacks oxygen. There are no molluscs, such as snails, because these creatures require alkaline, calcium-rich waters to make their shells. The most abundant species are insects, particularly mosquitoes.

The temperature of the northern bogs is usually too cold for reptiles and some amphibians. Frogs are found widely, however, except in the far north. They provide the chief source of food for the main bird predator, the crane.

Mammals are scarce in bog regions. In northern Canada, for example, only two species are plentiful, the beaver and the muskrat.

SALTMARSH

It is late October on the saltmarshes of East Anglia in eastern England. And the dark Brent geese are flying in to their winter feeding grounds. They come in low over the sea in long straggly lines and descend on the wetland recently flooded by the tide. They will remain here, feeding on the lush eel-grass, until the spring. Then they will fly north, back to their Arctic breeding grounds.

Marshes occur near the sea coasts in East Anglia and in many other parts of the world. They become extensive in shallow river deltas, where the rivers have deposited fertile sediment, but, as they are regularly flooded by seawater, only plant species that can tolerate salt can survive. In tropical regions the salty tidal swamps are thickly populated by mangrove trees and form mangrove swamps (see page 68–9). In temperate regions where grasses are the main kind of vegetation they are called saltmarshes.

In some saltmarshes there are varieties of reeds and bulrushes similar to those found in freshwater wetlands. In others the main plants are grasses, such as eel-grass, chord grass and salt hay. Other plants that tolerate salt may also be found. They include glasswort, so called because it was once used in glassmaking, Sea lavender and Sea purslane. Plants that can live in salty conditions are known as halophytes. Many contain special glands for getting rid of excess salt in their tissues.

LIFE IN THE MARSHES

Few mammals inhabit the saltmarshes because of the nature of the ground. Occasionally small mammals such as rabbits may feed on the plants when the tide goes out. Invertebrates such as worms, crustaceans and insects are the chief land animals of the marshes. They provide food for a wide variety of bird life, particularly wading birds.

THE WADERS

The common wading birds found on the marshes include the redshank, curlew, dunlin, godwit and oyster-catcher. Among the most distinctive feature of the birds is their bill. Most waders have a relatively longer bill than most other birds and they use it to probe into the mud for prey.

The curlew has the longest bill (up to 8in) and it curves downwards. Curlews also have long legs, so they can feed in deeper waters than most other waders. Touch-sensitive regions near the tip of their bills help them to locate their prey. Birds with a short bill, like the stint, feed at the surface, locating prey by sight.

MIGRANTS

Waders congregate on the saltmarshes and estuaries in the greatest numbers in winter. They are joined there by other birds that live inland for most of the year.

Great flocks of migrants also fly in from their breeding grounds in the far north to escape the severe cold of the Arctic winter. Some of these migrants fly very long distances. The Sharp-tailed sandpiper, for example, breeds in Siberia, but migrates as far south as Australasia for the winter.

◀A river carries large quantities of suspended mineral and organic matter. When it reaches the sea this matter is deposited as muddy silt. Extensive mud flats and marshes build up in river estuaries.

The saltmarshes are also the wintering grounds for many species of geese, which breed on the Arctic tundra. They include the small dark-colored Brent goose and the larger deep-brown Bean goose. The preferred food of the Brent goose is eel-grass, while that of the Bean goose is the roots of Sea club rush.

▶A Marbled godwit probes for worms in the soft mud as the tide goes out. It breeds in northern Canada and winters along coasts as far south as Peru.

▼Brent geese feed on eel-grasses on a saltmarsh in eastern England. Each winter the geese migrate south from the Arctic to saltmarshes all along North Sea coasts.

MANGROVES

A fly settles on a leaf about 3ft above the water in a mangrove swamp in Java. Its eyes keep watch for danger from above. But danger lurks below in the water, where an Archer fish is swimming by. The fish comes to the surface and "spits" drops of water into the air. Its aim is good, and the drops knock the fly into the water.

When rivers reach the sea coast, the sediment they carry settles out to form muddy wetlands. In tropical regions, such as Java in South-east Asia, the wetlands soon become colonized by mangrove trees.

There are several kinds of mangroves, but they all have a similar life style. They send down roots from their trunks and branches into the mud below. New trunks grow up from where the roots reach the ground, making a dense thicket.

For much of the time the roots of the mangroves are underneath the salty water. This would kill the roots of ordinary trees because they would not be able to breathe. Mangroves survive because their roots can take in air directly through their aerial roots, which are called pneumatophores.

MANGROVE LIFE
In most mangrove swamps fresh mud is continually being deposited by the river. This provides nourishment for

many invertebrates, such as worms, molluscs and crustaceans, such as crabs. Fiddler crabs scavenge on the exposed mud. They are often territorial and use their over-sized claw to gesticulate at their neighbors.

Invertebrates provide food for a variety of birds, such as the Scarlet ibis. The waters lapping the mangrove roots teem with fish, which are food for birds like the darter. Darters are also known as snakebirds because they often swim with just their long snake-like neck showing above water.

The strangest fish of the mangroves is the mudskipper. It often climbs out of the water at low tide and clings to mangrove roots. Unusually for a fish, it can breathe in the air.

Mammals are generally absent from the ground in mangrove swamps. But in some areas monkeys live in the leafy canopy. The biggest animal at sea level is the crocodile, a fierce predator that will attack any animal that comes within reach.

◀▼Animals of mangrove swamps from different parts of the world Mangrove winkle (*Littorina scabra*) (1) from the Seychelle Islands. Soldier crab (*Dotilla mictyroides*) (2) and Archer fish (*Toxotes jaculator*) (3) from South-east Asia. Proboscis monkey (*Nasalis larvatus*) (4) from Borneo. Great egret (*Egretta alba*) (5), common in all mangrove swamps. American darter or anhinga (*Anhinga anhinga*) (6) and the Scarlet ibis (*Eudocimus ruber*) (7) from the Americas. Saltwater crocodile (*Crocodylus porosus*) (8) from South-east Asia and northern Australia. The mudskipper (*Periophthalmus* species) (9) from South-east Asia.

SHORELINE

The starfish "smells" there is a meal nearby. It is a mussel, which has snapped the two halves of its shell tightly shut. But this is no defense against the starfish. It climbs over the mussel and uses the suckers on its feet to pull the two halves of the shell apart. Then it thrusts in its stomach tissue and begins to feed.

Starfish and mussels live in one of the most difficult habitats for living things – the intertidal region. This is the part of the seashore over which the tide ebbs and flows twice a day. Organisms that live in this region must be able to live underwater for some of the time, and in the air for the rest. They must also be able to stand up to the pounding of the waves. It might be thought that few species could survive in such a seemingly hostile environ-

ment, but in fact the seashore is often remarkably rich in life.

No land-based animals can survive underwater for an extended period, so most of the life in the intertidal region is marine. The main problem then for these marine species is to avoid drying out in the air.

PLANTS ON ROCKY SHORES
Rocky shores and sandy or muddy shores support different kinds of

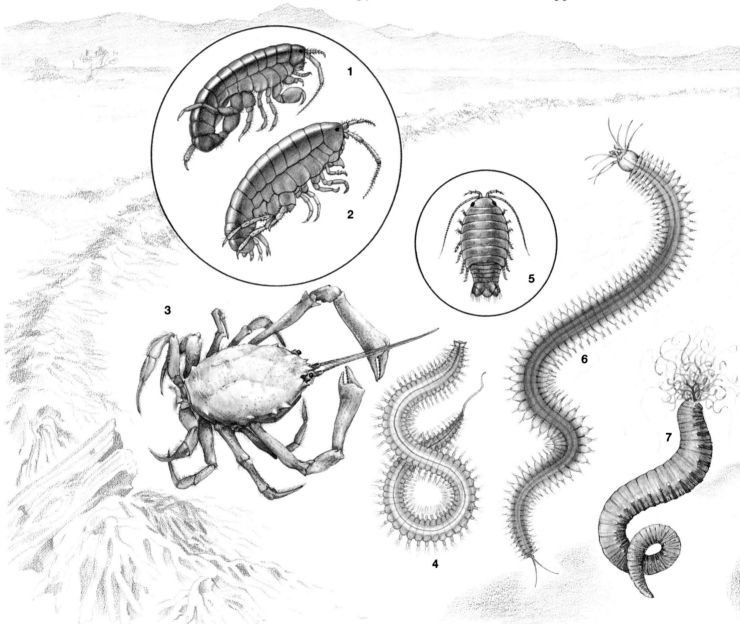

plants and animals. A major feature of rocky shores is the seaweed growing on the seabed and rocks. Seaweeds are simple plants called algae. Most of those in cool and temperate waters are brown. Those in warm tropical waters are usually red or green.

Among the common seaweeds are the kelps and wracks. The kelps are large plants that grow mainly at or below the low-tide level, in the sub-littoral zone. The wracks are found higher up in the mid-shore, or eulit-toral zone. Their rubbery leaves do not dry out as quickly as those of the kelp. Some wracks grow even beyond the ordinary high-tide level in the littoral zone.

LIVING IN A SHELL
The commonest kind of animals on rocky shores are molluscs, whose shells help to prevent their bodies drying when the tide goes out. They

◄▼**Animals that live on sandy shores in north-western Europe** Sandhoppers (e.g. *Orchestia gammarella, Talitrus saltator*) (1, 2). At the high-tide level: on the upper shore: the Masked crab (*Corystes cassivelaunus*) (3), polychaete worms (*Nephtys caeca*) (4) and isopods (*Eurydice pulchra*) (5). On the mid-shore: the ragworm (*Nereis diversicolor*) (6), another polychaete worm (*Amphitrite johnstoni*) (7), the Sand mason (*Lanice conchilega*) (8) and the Peacock worm (*Sabella pavonina*) (9). On the lower shore: the Sea potato (*Echinocardium cordatum*) (10), the Common otter shell (*Lutraria lutraria*) (11), the Pod razor shell (*Ensis siliqua*) (12), and tellins (e.g. *Tellina tenuis, Tellina fabula*) (13, 14).

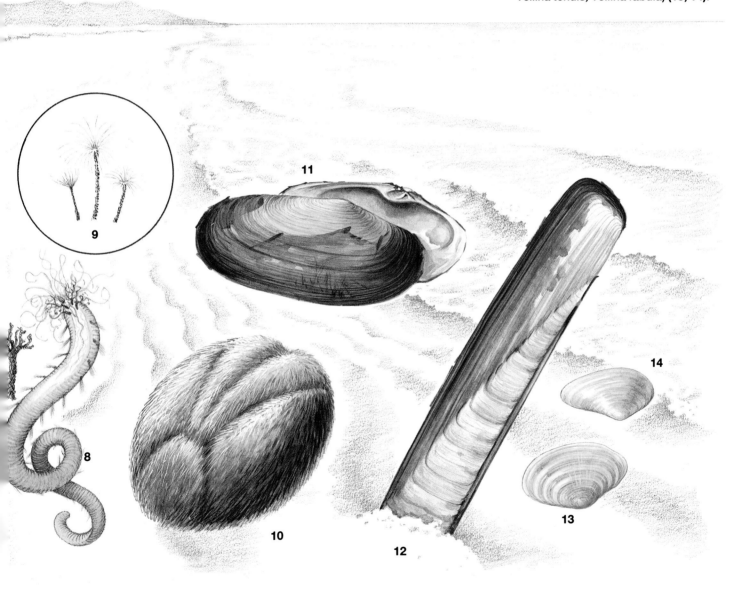

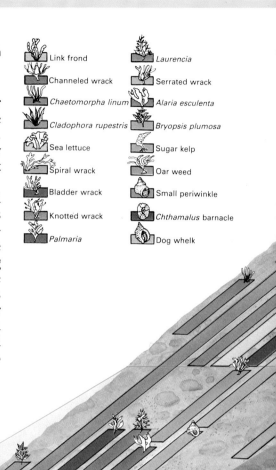

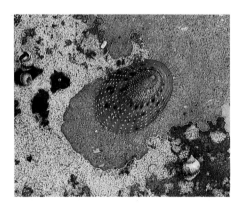

▲Sea anemones are found in many rock pools. The incoming tide brings in a fresh supply of food twice a day.

either close their shells tightly shut or they clamp them to a rock. Typical are limpets, winkles, mussels and whelks. Barnacles are also common on rocky shores. They look like molluscs, but are in fact crustaceans.

Many molluscs, like the limpet, feed on the tiny algae that coat the rocks and often the large seaweeds. Barnacles feed in a different way. They are filter-feeders, which extend long "legs" to catch plankton and minute animals floating in the water. Mussels are also filter-feeders. They take water inside their shells through siphon tubes. Food particles are then filtered out by gills, which the molluscs also use for breathing.

Link frond
Channeled wrack
Chaetomorpha linum
Cladophora rupestris
Sea lettuce
Spiral wrack
Bladder wrack
Knotted wrack
Palmaria
Laurencia
Serrated wrack
Alaria esculenta
Bryopsis plumosa
Sugar kelp
Oar weed
Small periwinkle
Chthamalus barnacle
Dog whelk

Sublittoral   Averag
Extreme low tide

▼Molluscs such as limpets use their rasp-like tongue to graze on the algae that coat the rocks in the tidal region.

Whelks are carnivores that prey on other molluscs. To help them find their prey they have a siphon that directs water over their taste cells. Dog whelks are mobile and prey mainly on molluscs or barnacles that are sedentary, or fixed. The Dog whelk is able to bore through the shells of molluscs to get at their flesh.

ROCK POOLS
Animals that cannot live for long out of water shelter under boulders, or they find crevices and damp overhangs in the rocks, or they inhabit the tidal pools on rocky shores. They

include sea anemones, crabs, sea urchins, shrimps and starfishes.

ON SANDY AND MUDDY SHORES
These shores support quite different forms of life. The shifting nature of the shorebed means that seaweeds cannot gain a footing. Animals that graze on plants are therefore absent. The basic food sources for shoreline creatures are tiny algae that cling to grains of sand, and plankton that come in with the tide. The tide also brings in a variety of other edible matter, such as seaweed and dead fish and other creatures. On muddy

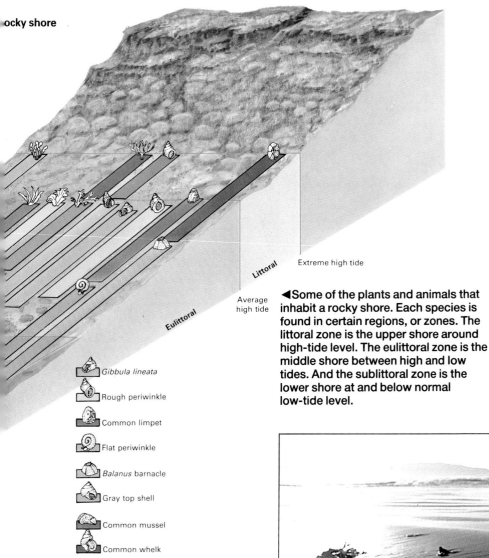

Rocky shore

Extreme high tide

Littoral

Average high tide

Eulittoral

Gibbula lineata

Rough periwinkle

Common limpet

Flat periwinkle

Balanus barnacle

Gray top shell

Common mussel

Common whelk

◄Some of the plants and animals that inhabit a rocky shore. Each species is found in certain regions, or zones. The littoral zone is the upper shore around high-tide level. The eulittoral zone is the middle shore between high and low tides. And the sublittoral zone is the lower shore at and below normal low-tide level.

shores around estuaries an additional supply of food is deposited by the outflowing river.

The main life on sandy and muddy shores lives under the surface. This includes a wide variety of marine worms, called polychaetes, such as lugworms and ragworms. These feed on minute plant and animal matter in the sand. The polychaetes known as fan worms have a fan-like crown of filaments on the head. They use the crown for breathing and filtering food from the water. Various molluscs, including clams, are able to burrow into the shorebed.

Crustaceans such as sandhoppers and crabs are active on the surface throughout the tidal region. So are many species of wading birds, from the tiny sandpipers to the large curlews and avocets.

▼A jellyfish lies stranded on the shore when the tide goes out. Before the tide comes in again, it will be dead.

▼Many kinds of crabs scavenge for food on the seashore, feeding on detritus and the remains of dead sea creatures.

OCEANS

A clownfish is swimming in the shallow waters off the Australian coast. It is keeping close to the seabed, which is covered with large sea anemones, whose colorful tentacles wave about in the current. And it never strays far from one particular anenome. The clownfish is only about 2in long, and is easy prey for larger fish. When one comes near, it dashes into the tentacles of the anenome. With many fish, this would mean death as the tentacles carry stinging cells. But this clownfish is unharmed because it has an association with this particular anenome.

▶ These small crustaceans are called krill; they provide food for many species of fish and the great baleen whales.

▼ The underside of a Common or Moon jellyfish, which is found in large numbers in the North Atlantic.

Life began in the oceans and is still found there in greatest variety. It is richest in the warmer, shallower waters of the continental shelves which surround Australia and the other great land masses. Yet it can still be found even in the ocean deeps, where daylight never reaches and the pressure is enormous. The oceans cover more than two-thirds of the world's surface to an average depth of over 2mi. In places there are chasms 7mi deep.

The basic food source is the minute plant life called phytoplankton. This consists of single-celled algae, which live in the top 300ft or so of the sea, where there is plenty of light. The plankton need the light to make their food by photosynthesis. Many kinds of multi-celled algae, or seaweed, are a source of food for marine life.

MICROSCOPIC PREY

The phytoplankton provide food for a wide variety of tiny "grazing" animals, the zooplankton. The most abundant of these are primitive crustaceans called copepods and the larger krill. The larvae of other marine life – worms, molluscs and fish – also make up the zooplankton.

The copepods and krill in turn provide food for ocean carnivores, small and large. Among these are jellyfishes, found in most oceans. They use stinging tentacles to immobilize their prey, which can also include small fish. Small squid feed on copepods and krill. So do many fish, including herring and mackerel and

▶ A close-up photo of a sea anemone on the Great Barrier Reef in Australia, showing the tentacles and mouth area.

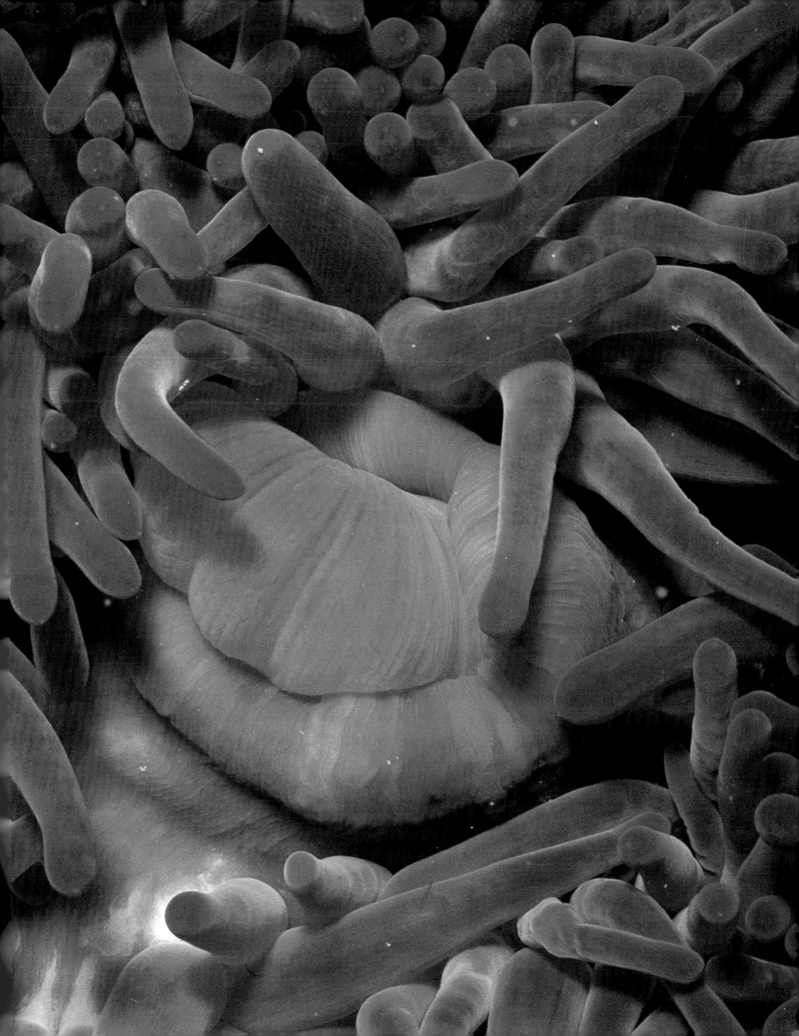

the large manta rays and basking sharks. The huge baleen whales also have a similar diet.

THE NOTORIOUS SHARK

Among the larger marine predators sharks are the best known. Many feed on small fish but others eat almost anything living that comes their way. The notorious Great white shark is one of the most deadly. It is also sometimes called the maneater because it does occasionally attack humans. But its usual diet is sea mammals, such as porpoises and seals. It grows to a length of 23ft, somewhat larger than another fierce predator, the Tiger shark.

ILLUMINATING THE ABYSS

Some of the most curious fish in the oceans exist at great depths, 6,500ft or more, in the so-called abyssal zone. At such depths no light penetrates, so it is always dark. Some fish, such as the deep-sea anglers, carry luminous lures on the head to attract prey to them. Most have vicious-looking inward-curving teeth, which allow prey to enter easily, but prevent them coming out again. This is just one adaptation to make sure they hold on to prey, which are scarce in the ocean depths.

▲Life on a coral reef is rich and varied, from exquisitely colored sea slugs and butterfly fish to this fierce Great white shark. The reefs are formed from the chalky skeletons of corals. Corals are primitive filter-feeding animals closely related to sea anemones.

▼Two butterfly fish flit around a coral reef. Their banded coloring provides camouflage while the black eye band and false eye spot on the dorsal fin helps to confuse would-be predators. Coral reefs are found in warm, shallow tropical seas such as the Red Sea.

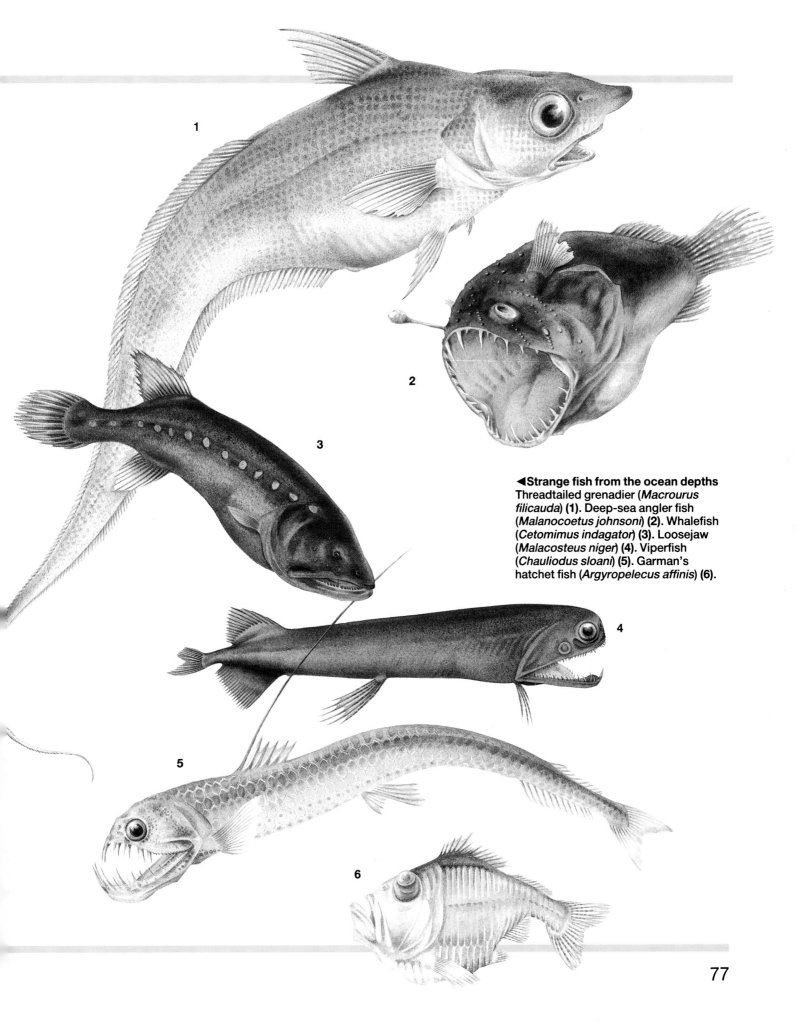

◀**Strange fish from the ocean depths**
Threadtailed grenadier (*Macrourus filicauda*) (1). Deep-sea angler fish (*Malanocoetus johnsoni*) (2). Whalefish (*Cetomimus indagator*) (3). Loosejaw (*Malacosteus niger*) (4). Viperfish (*Chauliodus sloani*) (5). Garman's hatchet fish (*Argyropelecus affinis*) (6).

► ▼ **Typical features of seals and the walrus** The Harbor seal (*Phoca vitulina*) **(1a)**, a hair seal, has sleek hair and no ear flaps. It is cumbersome on land **(1b)**. The Cape fur seal (*Arcocephalus pusillus*) **(2a)** is a typical eared seal, with ear flaps and thick fur. On land it supports itself on its flippers **(2b)**. The walrus (*Odobenus rosmarus*) **(3a)** has long tusks. It stands and walks on land on all four limbs **(3b)**.

LOW LIFE

A fascinating variety of animals live on or near the seabed. Among the lowly life there are filter-feeders like barnacles and sponges, which prefer to live on rocky seabeds. On sandy seabeds, animals that feed on detritus, or organic matter falling from above, often dominate. They include numerous polychaete worms, molluscs and crustaceans.

Many kinds of fish prey on the invertebrates, including flatfish such as plaice. The plaice, like other flatfish, is totally adapted to life on the seabed. It has a flattened body with both eyes on the same side of its head.

One of the largest predators is a mollusc, the octopus, named after its eight tentacles. It spends most time in rock crevices, emerging only to chase prey that comes near. Another crevice-dweller is the Moray eel, which has blunt, rounded teeth to crush the crabs that form the main part of its diet.

OCEAN MAMMALS

The largest animals found in the sea are whales. Unlike fish and most other marine life, they are warm-blooded. They are mammals, and like land mammals they breathe air into their lungs. The females give birth to live young, which suckle their milk.

Whales are not the only marine mammals. Dolphins, porpoises, seals, walruses and sea lions are mammals too. Whales, dolphins and porpoises spend all of their time in the water. Seals, walruses and sea lions usually feed in the water, but spend some of their time on land, mainly to breed.

The diet of the sea mammals varies from species to species. The largest whales, such as the 90ft-long Blue whale, are filter-feeders, straining plankton and krill from the water with the comb-like plates of baleen in their mouth. Other whales, for instance the Sperm whale, feed on fish, squid and crustaceans. The Killer whale attacks penguins, seals and other whales.

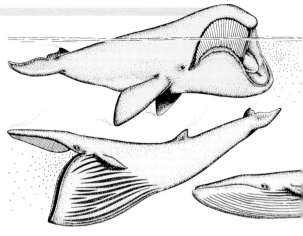

▲Baleen whales use different techniques to filter food through their baleen plates. Right whales (top) filter food by swimming forwards with their mouths open. Rorquals (like the Blue whale) take a mouthful of water and then force it out through the baleen.

▼A Humpback whale feeding at the surface. It is taking a mouthful of water and is about to close its mouth. Then it will expel the water through the comb-like baleen on its upper jaw, leaving any food inside its mouth.

ISLANDS

The two leathery eggs were laid about 10 days ago, and now they are hatching underneath an animal that is neither a reptile nor a bird. It has a fur-covered body rather like an otter, but instead of an otter-like head, it has a broad flat bill rather like a duck. The newly hatched young are tiny, pink and naked. They crawl slowly through the fur on their mother's belly up to glands that soon start to ooze milk. They begin to suckle. This animal is a platypus, a mammal that lays eggs.

▼A rugged coral island, near Tahiti in the South Pacific Ocean. Isolated islands often have distinct species of animals.

The platypus is one of the unique forms of life that developed in Australia. It is a primitive kind of mammal, which might have been expected to die out when more advanced mammals evolved. The main reason it did not die out was that Australia is an island. Many islands have species that have uniquely survived from earlier times. Exactly which species they are depends on when the island separated from the mainland.

Australia became an island some 45 million years ago, when it split away from what is now Antarctica. It contained no advanced mammals at that time, and the surrounding sea then prevented advanced mammals migrating to it. With no competition for its river habitat, the platypus survived.

Australia's other unique animal species – kangaroos, koalas and other

marsupials – survived for the same reason. They are also primitive mammals, which raise their young in pouches. They would not have thrived in competition with placental mammals, whose offspring are born more fully developed.

MARSUPIAL NICHES
Marsupials probably originated in South America, and many species are still found there today. But they are different from the Australian species because they have had to face competition from advanced mammals coming from North America.

For example, the introduction of fierce big cats like jaguars led to the extinction of large carnivorous marsupials in South America. Most of the marsupials remaining, such as the Common and mouse opossums, are

omnivores, feeding on fruit, insects, worms and various small animals.

In Australia various species of marsupials have evolved in parallel with placental mammals elsewhere to fill similar ecological niches. Thus, the carnivorous Tasmanian wolf evolved with a similar physical form to the placental wolf on other continents. And the Marsupial mole developed the same body form as the placental mole, and both have the same burrowing habit. This kind of parallel development is called convergent evolution.

▶Male kangaroos fighting over a female on heat. Kangaroos are just one of Australia's many unique species.

▼Giant tortoises on the Galapagos Islands. With no enemies, they grew to great size, with only a thin shell.

▲Two rare animals peculiar to the island of Madagascar. The falanouc (top) has an elongated snout and body and feeds on worms and other invertebrates. The fanaloka (bottom) is more fox-like and eats lizards, frogs and rodents.

81

ON MADAGASCAR

The island of Madagascar lies in the Indian Ocean off the coast of East Africa. The main mammal species on the island are the lemurs, which are found nowhere else. These animals are called prosimians, which means they evolved before the simians – the monkeys and apes. Their ancestors lived in mainland Africa when Madagascar separated about 50 million years ago.

On the mainland these ancestors were eventually replaced by the more advanced monkeys and apes. But on Madagascar no monkeys or apes evolved or could reach the island from outside so the lemur ancestors filled the kinds of niches monkeys and apes fill elsewhere.

ON THE GALAPAGOS ISLANDS

The Galapagos Islands are located near the equator about 625mi off Ecuador, the country to which they

belong. Two distinct forms of animal life have evolved on these isolated islands. Among the largest creatures are the land and marine iguanas and the giant tortoises. Even on separate islands within the Galapagos group the tortoises have developed differences, for example in the pattern of their shell.

The islands are populated by a variety of finches. These evolved from finches that were somehow blown to the islands from the mainland. On the mainland the finches occupied a seed-eating niche among the native birds.

On the islands, however, there was no competition from other birds, so the finches were able to exploit the other food sources. Eventually they evolved different bills to cope with the different foods. For example, some finches have a short, slim bill like a flycatcher's, for eating insects. Others have a thick bill like a parrot's, for cracking nuts.

FLIGHTLESS ISLAND BIRDS

The water around islands is no barrier to birds, which can fly across it, but it is a barrier to larger animals. The result is that the birds often find they have no predators. With no need to escape from predators, some birds lose their ability to fly.

The takahe and kiwi of New Zealand are examples of flightless island birds that still survive. Some have not been so fortunate. They include the moa, also from New Zealand, and the famous dodo, which came from Mauritius. Both these birds were hunted to extinction by those most deadly predators – people.

◄The takahe of New Zealand, a flightless bird of the rail group. The bird is now in danger of extinction because of predators introduced by people.

►A Ring-tailed lemur leaps into the air, with tail outstretched to steady itself. It also uses its tail, smeared with scent, to signal to other lemurs.

FARMLAND

A tiny furry acrobat is using her feet and tail to climb the stiff stalks of ripening wheat. She twists her tail around the stalks to save herself should she fall. This hungry female Harvest mouse spots a weevil and chews that up before it starts on the swollen ears of grain. Then, with her hunger satisfied, she scuttles into the tall grass at the edge of the field. Here she climbs up to her neat spherical nest woven around the grass stems. Inside are six hairless young. They come to life as their mother settles down, blindly search for and find, a teat on her belly and start to suckle.

▲A crop of oil-seed rape in flower. Growing the same kind of plant over vast areas all but eliminates native plant species and the varied animal life that depend on them.

▼**Some animals that have thrived on farming** The Red kangaroo (*Macropus rufus*) **(1)** in Australian grasslands. The Virginia opossum (*Didelphis virginiana*) **(2)** in North America. The Asian white-backed vulture (*Gyps bengalensis*) **(3)**. The Harvest mouse (*Micromys minutus*) **(4)** and Red-legged partridge (*Alectoris rufa*) **(5)** in European wheatfields. The Paddyfield warbler (*Acrocephalus agricola*) **(6)** and Chinese pond heron (*Ardeola bacchus*) **(7)** in South-east Asia. The Cane rat (*Thryonomys gregorianus*) **(8)** in Africa.

2

1

3

Harvest mice now thrive on farm crops, but before about 10,000 years ago, humans had little effect on the environment. They gathered fruits, nuts and roots to eat, like many other animals. They also hunted for meat as do many animal predators.

But around 8,000 BC things began to change. People started to live a more settled life, growing crops and herding sheep and goats so they did not have to hunt so often for meat.

To grow crops well, the new farmers often had to clear forest land and scrub by cutting (slashing) and burning. They changed their environment, and thus began to upset the natural communities of plants and animals. This process has been going on ever since.

GRAIN LOVERS

This man-made biome is often called the agricultural biome, or agribiome. It is a simple biome because farmers grow a limited number of crops in a given area. By concentrating on just a few crops, particularly cereals, farmers create a very particular type of habitat, which can support only limited wildlife. Certain species, however, thrive in agribiomes. It has been so since the days when farming began and rats and mice were attracted to the first great grain stores in the Middle East.

AGRICULTURAL POISONS

To make sure that their crops grow well, farmers feed the soil with fertilizers, and spray the crops with herbicides and pesticides. The herbicides kill off plants that compete with the crop. The pesticides kill pests and diseases that reduce the crop yield. However, these chemicals may harm beneficial creatures as well as pests, and may make their way into the wildlife food chain. For example, birds are killed by the pesticides consumed by the mice they prey on.

Modern chemical farming methods pose a risk to the environment, and so too does the ages-old method of slash and burn. This is now being practised over vast areas of the rain forests where it is destroying the habitats of many of the world's most exotic and unique flora and fauna.

CITY AND TOWN

It is long past midnight in the suburbs of an English town. A terrible scream rings out, but it is not a person screaming. It is a Red fox vixen calling to her mate. This pair of foxes have taken up residence in the area, making a den under an old shed in a neglected garden. They are foraging for food. One is nosing among the scraps on a compost heap in a nearby garden. The other is playing tug of war with a large worm that has come to the surface of the lawn.

Foxes are perhaps not the kind of wildlife one would expect to see in towns. But they are becoming increasingly common, particularly in Britain. They not only feed in suburban gardens, they also breed there. Many other animals have also learned to take advantage of the man-made environment of the city, which is often called the urban biome.

The city provides a habitat quite unlike anything else found in nature. Most of the ground is covered with concrete, tarmac or buildings. This all acts as a heat store, warming the local climate by several degrees. The city is also very noisy, and is full of dust and

fumes from thousands of vehicles. And, of course, it is full of people.

The urban biome would thus not appear to be attractive to any wildlife at all! But it turns out in practice to be remarkably rich in species that have learned to live with people in this environment.

LOADS OF GARBAGE

The main thing that attracts many species of animals to cities and the surrounding areas is the waste human beings create. This is thrown into the streets, stuffed into trash cans which are easily knocked over, and dumped on garbage heaps. It provides a plentiful food supply for wildlife.

Raccoons, jackals, coyotes, foxes and opossums are some of the animals that venture into the streets in different parts of the world to raid discarded waste and trash cans. Rats are common everywhere, often living in the drains and sewers beneath the streets and in buildings.

The large garbage heaps on the edge of many towns attract an equally varied range of animals. In some areas

◄The Red fox has taken up residence in many cities and thrives there. Its main diet consists of food scavenged from compost heaps and trash cans.

in North America Brown bears are now common visitors, while in Arctic towns Polar bears have appeared. Sometimes the bears stray into town, bringing them into conflict with the human population.

Many kinds of birds also scavenge on the garbage heaps. In many parts of Europe large flocks of gulls descend on them, particularly Herring gulls and Black-headed gulls. Garbage scavengers in other parts of the world include the Polar bear in the Arctic, and Black vulture in the Americas and the Marabou stork in Africa.

CITY BIRDS

Buildings in the city provide nesting and roosting sites for many birds. Feral pigeons are perhaps the most common. They are varieties of Rock dove that have descended from once-domesticated birds. They nest on ledges among the buildings, which are

◄A Common kestrel perches on a highway bridge. The green verges of highways are a haven for small animals, good prey for the kestrel.

▼The Gray squirrel has so successfully adapted to urban life that it has become a pest in many areas. It will drive away other wildlife and eat their food supply.

a good substitute for their ancestral nesting sites in rocks and cliffs.

Similar sites are chosen by the occasional birds of prey in the city, such as kestrels. These birds prey mainly on another common city bird, the House sparrow. The sparrow, originally a grain-eater, was first attracted to city streets in the days when horses were common, feeding on the grain from their nosebags.

UNWELCOME GUESTS

Many smaller creatures live inside buildings. House mice are common, as are their larger cousins, rats. Rats in particular do enormous damage, gnawing through packaging, cables and wooden structures, and leaving droppings that are a source of disease.

Among insects, cockroaches are perhaps the most unwelcome residents. They are often termed the rats and mice of the insect world, for they have thrived in association with man. They are found particularly in food shops, stores and kitchens. Three species have become widespread pests, the American, German and Oriental cockroaches. They are mainly nocturnal, long-lived, wary and difficult to get rid of.

OPEN SPACES

Most cities usually have areas of open ground, such as formal gardens and parks, often with ponds. The flora will usually include trees, together with a wide variety of flowering shrubs and plants. These plants will attract and

support all kinds of insects, which in turn will attract birds and other wildlife. Weed plants colonize waste ground wherever it occurs.

Rivers, canals, reservoirs and lakes provide homes for many kinds of aquatic species. Ducks, coots, gulls and the moorhen all fly in to join pelicans and other imported birds in city parks.

In the suburbs the patchwork of gardens provides a rich habitat for wildlife of every description – foxes and hedgehogs, voles and moles, squirrels and beetles, and birds and butterflies of every hue. Gardens can be a haven for many animals. More species of butterfly are to be found in West African gardens than in nearby tropical rain forests.

▼Various animals attracted by city waste The Common raccoon (*Procyon lotor*) (1). The House mouse (*Mus musculus*) (2). The Norway rat (*Rattus norvegicus*) (3).The Herring gull (*Larus argentatus*) (4) and Black-headed gull (*L. ridibundus*) (5).

▲▼**Urban birds and insects** The Feral pigeon (*Columba livia*) **(1)** and House sparrow (*Passer domesticus*) **(2)** roost on city buildings and scavenge on the streets. The Common starling (*Sturnus vulgaris*) **(3)** often flies in to roost at night. Waste-ground plants attract butterflies like the Small white (*Pieris rapae*) **(4)**. The Oriental cockroach (*Blatta orientalis*) **(5)** is an unwelcome insect pest.

▼This Song thrush has built its nest in a storeroom. When natural habitats are lacking, animals have to improvize.

GLOSSARY

Adaptation Features of an animal's body or life-style that suit it to its environment.

Aestivation (also **estivation**) Summer sleep to avoid the heat.

Alpine Belonging to the Alps or other high mountains.

Amphibians Animals such as frogs and toads, which have a larval stage dependent on water and an adult stage that lives on land.

Antarctic The bitterly cold region around the South Pole.

Aquatic Living for much, if not all, of the time in the water.

Arboreal Living for much, if not all, of the time in the trees.

Arctic The bitterly cold region around the North Pole.

Biome A major ecological unit that has characteristic plant and animal life, closely related to climate – for example savannah grassland.

Big cats Large carnivores of the cat family, such as lions, tigers, leopards and cheetahs.

Bog A usually cold wetland on peaty soils, which has little animal life.

Boreal Of the north.

Browser An animal that feeds on the shoots, leaves and bark of shrubs and trees.

Camouflage Color and patterns on an animal's coat that allow it to blend in with its surroundings.

Canids Animals that belong to the dog family, such as jackals, wolves and foxes.

Canopy The upper living layer of a forest formed by the intermingling of branches and leaves.

Carnivore A meat-eater.

Carrion Meat from a dead animal.

Chapparal The large area of scrubland in California.

Climate The average weather conditions in a region.

Colonization The process whereby new species take over a new habitat.

Competition The contest between two or more species over such things as space and food.

Conifers Trees that bear cones. Their needle-like leaves usually stay on the trees all year.

Coterie The name of the social group of prairie dogs.

Crustaceans Creatures with jointed limbs and a hard outer skin, like shrimp and krill.

Deciduous trees Trees that shed their leaves seasonally, usually in the autumn of fall.

Desert An area with low rainfall.

Detritivore An animal that feeds on detritus, that is, on plant and animal remains.

Diurnal Active during the day.

Dormant Resting or sleeping.

Ecology The study of plants and animals in relation to their environment.

Endangered species One that is in danger of becoming extinct.

Endemic A species that is native to a certain area.

Environment The surroundings of an organism, including both the living and non-living world.

Estuary The broad mouth of a river where it meets the sea.

Eutrophication The enrichment of water by nutrients, often the excess nitogenous fertilizers that run off farmland.

Extinction The complete loss of a species, locally or worldwide.

Fauna Animal life.

Feral Living in the wild. It refers to domesticated species or to animals that have escaped from captivity.

Flora Plant life.

Food web The feeding connections in a given community of animals and plants; literally who eats what.

Foraging Going in search of food.

Garrigue Sparse scrubland found in the Mediterranean region.

Genus The division of animal classification below Family and above Species.

Grazer An animal that feeds on grass.

Habitat The kind of surroundings in which an animal or plant lives.

Herbivore A plant-eater.

Hibernation Winter sleep to avoid the cold.

Incubation Period during which an animal keeps an egg warm, allowing the embryo inside to grow.

Insectivore An insect-eater.

Invertebrates Animals without a backbone.

Larva Plural larvae; an early stage in the life-cycle of an animal, for example of an insect or amphibian.

Llanos A region of tropical grassland in South America, south of the rain forests.

Mallee Scrubland in south Australia.

Mammal A class of animals whose females have mammary glands, which produce milk on which they feed their young.

Mangrove forest One that develops on the muddy shores of the sea in deltas and estuaries in the tropics.

Maquis Thick scrubland of the Mediterranean region.

Marine Living in or on the sea.

Marsh A wetland where the main plants are grasses.

Marsupial A class of primitive mammals, whose females give birth to very underdeveloped young and raise them (usually) in a pouch.

Mattoral Scrubland found in Chile, in South America.

Metamorphosis The change in the structure of an animal as it goes through its life-cycle, for example from egg to pupa to adult in insects.

Migration The movement of animals, especially movement over a long distance, for the purpose of feeding or breeding.

Molluscs Animals that usually have a shell, such as snails.

Nekton Free-swimming animals.

Niche The particular way of life of a species in a certain habitat, for example a leaf-eater in a rain forest.

Nocturnal Active during the night.

Nomadic Leading a wandering life.

Omnivore An animal with a varied diet, which eats both plants and animals.

Pampas The temperate grassland regions of South America.

Photosynthesis The process by which green plants are able to make their own food. They use the energy in sunlight and chlorophyll in their leaves to combine carbon dioxide (from the air) with water (from the ground) to make sugar.

Plankton Microscopic plants (phytoplankton) and animals (zooplankton) that live in water and drift with the current.

Prairie The temperate grassland regions of North America.

Predator An animal that hunts other animals for food.

Prey An animal that is hunted.

Primates An order of animals that includes monkeys, apes and humans.

Rain forest Tropical and sub-tropical forest that has plentiful rainfall all year round.

Reptiles Cold-blooded animals with a scaly skin, such as snakes, lizards crocodiles and tortoises.

Rodent A mammal belonging to the animal order that includes rats, mice and squirrels.

Saltmarsh A wetland area near the coast, which is flooded by salty sea water as the tide comes in.

Savannah Tropical grassland, found in Africa, South America and Australia.

Scavenger An animal that feeds on the remains of carcasses that others have abandoned.

Scrub An area of low, shrubby vegetation, usually hot and dry.

Species The division of animal classification below Genus. A group of animals with broadly similar body structure and characteristics and that can breed together.

Steppe The temperate grassland regions of Eurasia.

Swamp A wetland where the main plants are trees.

Temperate climate One that is not too hot and not too cold.

Terrestrial Spending most of the time on the ground.

Tropics Strictly, the region between latitudes 23½° north and south of the equator; a region of heat and humidity, with high rainfall.

Tundra The cold, barren, treeless landscape of far northern regions of the world.

Vertebrates Animals with a backbone.

Waders Birds of the marsh and seashore that feed in the shallow water.

Wetland An area where water lays on the surface, such as a swamp, marsh or bog.

INDEX

Page numbers in normal "roman" type indicate text entries. **Bold** numbers refer to captions to illustrations. Many of the entries refer to general animal types and not to individual species. Where the text relates to a species, the Latin name of that animal is given in brackets after the common name.

agouti (*Dasyprocta* genus) 17
alligator
    American (*Alligator mississippiensis*) **63**, 64
alpaca (*Lama pacos*) 52
anemones
    sea *see* sea anemones
angler
    Deep-sea (*Malanocoetus johnsoni*) 77
anglers
    deep-sea 76
    see also angler
anhinga (*Anhinga anhinga*) **69**
antechinus
    Brown (*Antechinus stuartii*) **7**
antelope-squirrel
    White-tailed (*Ammospermaphilus leucurus*) **29**
antelopes 40
ants
    army 14
    soldier 14
apes
    Old World 9
armadillo
    Great-banded (*Dasypus novemcinctus*) 41
avocet (*Recurvirostra* genus) 73

badger
    American (*Taxidea taxus*) 44
    Eurasian (*Meles meles*) **22**, 44
badgers 22, 44, **44**
    see also badger
barbel (*Barbus barbus*)56
barnacles 72, 79
bat
    False vampire (*Vampyrum spectrum*) **16**
    Fishing bulldog (*Noctilio leporinus*) **16**
    Fringe-lipped (*Trachops cirrhosus*) **16**

Mustache (*Pteronotus parnelli*) **16**
bear
    American black (*Ursus americanus*) 19
    Asian black (*Selenarctos thibetanus*) 19
    Brown *see* bear, Grizzly
    Grizzly (*Ursus arctos*) 30, 48, 87
    Polar (*Ursus maritimus*) 6, **12**, 48, **49**, 87
    Spectacled (*Tremarctos ornatus*) 19
bears 9
    see also bear
beaver
    American (*Castor canadensis*) 26
    Mountain (*Aplodontia rufa*) **6**
beavers 24, 65
    see also beaver
beetle
    Dung (*Scarabaeus aeratus*) **41**
    Tenebrionid (Tenebrionidae family) 32
beetles 22, 27, 88
    dung **41**
    see also beetle
bighorn
    American (*Ovis canadensis*) 51
birds 22, 88
    fruit-eating 17
    wading 66, 73
birds of paradise 17
birds of prey 44
bison
    American (*Bison bison*) 12, 42, **43**
    European (*Bison bonasus*) 44
blackflies 49
boatman
    Water (*Notoneta glauca*) **58**
bowerbird
    Regent (*Sericulus chrysocephalus*) **17**
budworm
    Spruce ( ) 27
buffalo
    American *see* bison, American
    Forest (*Synceros caffer*) **51**
bushmaster (*Lachesis muta*) 17
butterflies 22,88
    see also butterfly
butterfly
    Small white (*Pieris rapae*) **89**

buzzard (*Buteo buteo*) 48

caddisflies 55,60
caiman (*genus Caiman*) 62
camels 37
capuchin
    Brown (*Cebus apella*) **6**
capybara (*Hydrochoerus hydrochaeris*) 6, **6**, 62
caracal (*Felis caracal*) 35
caribou (*Rangifer tarandus*) 26, 46, 48, 49
    see also reindeer
cavies 9
centipedes 14
cheetah (*Acinonyx jubatus*) **38**, 41
chamois (*Rupicapra rupicapra*) 51
chevrotains 17
chinchillas (*genus Chinchilla*) 52
clams 55,73
clownfish (*Amphiprion* species) 74
cock
    chaparral *see* Road runner
cockroach
    American (*Periplaneta americana*) 88
    German (*Blatella germanica*) 88
    Oriental (*Blatta orientalis*) 88, **89**
cockroaches, 14,88
    see also cockroach
condor (*Vultur gryphus*) 53
coot (*Fulica atra*) 56,88
copepods 74
corals **76**
cougar *see* puma
coyote (*Canis latrans*) **27**, 42, 86
crab
    Masked (*Corystes cassivelaunus*) **71**
    Soldier (*Dotilla mictyroides*) **69**
crabs 69,72,73,73
    fiddler 69
    see also crab
cranes 65
crocodile
    Saltwater (*Crocodylus porosus*) **69**
crocodiles 64, 69
    see also crocodile
crossbill
    Red (*Loxia curvirostra*) **25**

crossbills 27
    see also crossbill
crustaceans 55, 58, 60, 66, 69, 72, 73, 75, 79
curlew (*Numenius arquata*) 66, 73
Cyclops 55

damselfly (*Coenagrion puella*) **55**, 60
Daphnia 60
darter
    American *see* anhinga
darters 69
    see also darter
deer 22
    Black-tailed *see* deer, Mule
    Mule (*Odocoileus hemionus*) **18**, 19, 30
    Pampas (*Ozotoceros bezoarticus*) 44
    Red (*Cervus elaphus*) **6**, **22**, **27**, 44
    Roe (*Capreolus capreolus*) **43**, 44
degu (*Octondon genus*) 30
devil
    Tasmanian (*Sarcophilus harrisii*) **7**
dingo (*Canis dingo*) 35
dipper
    American (*Cinclus mexicanus*) 54
dippers 54, 56
    see also dipper
dogs
    prairie *see* prairie dogs
    wild *see* wild dogs
dolphins 79
    river 56
donkeys 37
dormice 22
    see also dormouse
dormouse
    Common (*Muscardinus avellanarius*) **23**
dove
    Rock (*Columba livia*) 87
dragonflies 60
    (*Anisoptera* species)
duck
    Torrent (*Merganetta armata*) 56
    Tufted (*Aythya fuligula*) 58
ducks 56, 88
    see also duck
duiker (*Cephalophus rufilatus*) **51**
dunlin (*Calidris alpina*) 66

92

eagle
　Bald (*Haliaeetus leucocephalus*) 64
　Crowned (*Stephanoaetus coronatus*) 17
　Harpy (*Harpia harpyia*) 17
eagles 37
　see also eagle
echidnas 8
eel
　freshwater (genus *Anguilla*) 55
　moray 79
egret
　Cattle (*Bubulcus ibis*) **64**
　Great (*Egretta alba*) **69**
eland
　Common (*Taurotragus oryx*) 40
elephant 17
　African (*Loxodonta africana*) 11, **11**, 39
　Indian (*Elephas maximus bengalensis*) 11
elephants 9, 17, 40, **51**
elk *see* deer, Red
emu (*Dromaius novaehollandiae*) 37

falanouc (*Eupleres gondotii*) 81
falcon
　Peregrine (*Falco peregrinus*) **27**
falcons 48
　see also falcon
fanaloka (*Fossa fossa*) 81
fer de lance (*Bothrops* genus) 17
finches 82
fish
　Archer (*Toxotes jaculator*) 68, **69**
　butterfly **76**
fisher (*Martes pennanti*) 18
flamingo
　Greater (*Phoenicopterus ruber*) **64**
flamingos 64
　see also flamingo
flatworm (*Planaria* species) 58
fowl
　Mallee (*Leipoa ocellata*) 28, **30**
fox
　Arctic (*Alopex lagopus*) 48, **49**
　Fennec (*Vulpes zerda*) **35**
　Red (*Vulpes vulpes*) **6**, 86, **86**
foxes 9, 26,27,44,86,88
　see also fox

frog
　Common (*Rana temporaria*) **58**
frogs 60,63,65
　tree 17
　see also frog

gazelle
　Thomson (*Gazella thomsoni*) 40
gazelles 40
　see also gazelle
gecko (*Palmatogecko rangei*) **33**
geese 67
　see also goose
gerbils 34
gibbon
　Lar (*Hylobates lar*) **7**
Gila monster (*Heloderma suspectum*) 37
giraffe (*Giraffa camelopardalis*) **6**, 38, 40
gnu
　Brindled (*Connochaetes taurinus*) 40
gnus 40
　see also gnu
goat
　Angora (*Capra hircus aegagrus*) 52
goats 37
　see also goat
godwit
　Marbled (*Limosa fedoa*) 67
godwits 66
　see also godwit
goose
　Bean (*Branta bernicla*) 67
　Brent (*Anser fabalis*) 66, 67, **67**
　Canada (*Branta canadensis*) 49
　Graylag (*Anser anser*) 49
　White-Fronted (*Anser albifrons*) **46**, 49
gorilla (*Gorilla gorilla*) **6**, **6**, 11, 17
goshawks 24
grenadier
　Threadtailed (*Macrourus filicauda*) **77**
grylloblattids 53
guanaco (*Lama guanicoe*) 12, 44
gull
　Black-headed (*Larus ridibundus*) 87, **88**
　Herring (*L. argentatus*) 87, **88**

gulls 87,88
　see also gull

hamster
　Common (*Cricetus cricetus*) 44
hare
　Arctic (*Lepus timidus*) 48
　Snowshoe (*Lepus americanus*) 26, **27**
harrier
　Marsh (*Circus aeruginosus*) **64**
hatchet fish
　Garman's (*Argyropelecus affinis*) **77**
hawks 37
hedgehogs 20,22,88
hen
　Purple swamp (*Porphyrio porphyrio*) **64**
heron
　Black-crowned night (*Nycticorax nycticorax*) **64**
　Chinese pond (*Ardeola bacchus*) **84**
herons 56,60
　see also heron
herring (*Clupea harengus*) 74
hippopotamus (*Hippopotamus amphibius*) 56, 63
hornbills 17
hyena
　Striped (*Hyaena hyaena*) 35
hyenas 41
　see also hyena
hyrax
　Rock (genus *Procavia*) **51**

ibex (*Capra ibex*) 51, 52, **52**
ibis
　Scarlet (*Eudocimus ruber*) 69, **69**
iguana
　Barrington land **9**
　Marine (*Amblyrhynchus cristatus*) 82
iguanas 82
　see also iguana
impala (*Aepyceros melampus*) 40
insects 66
isopods (*Eurydice pulchra*) 71

jackal (*Canis aureus*) 41,86
jackrabbit
　Antelope (*Lepus alleni*) 29

jaegers 48
jaguar (*Panthera onca*) 6, **6**, 17
jaguars 9
　see also jaguar
jellyfish 73, 74
　Common (*Aurelia aurita*) 74
　Moon *see* jellyfish, Common
jerboas 35

kangaroo
　Eastern gray (*Macropus giganteus*) **7**
　Red (*Macropus rufus*) **84**
kangaroo-rat
　Merriam's (*Dipodomys merriomi*) **29**
kangaroo-rats 30, 35
　see also kangaroo-rat
kangaroos 8, 80, **81**
　see also kangaroo
kestrel
　Common (*Falco tinnunculus*) **87**
kestrels 88
　see also kestrel
kingfisher (*Alcedo atthis*) 56, 60
kiwi
　Great spotted (*Apteryx haastii*) **19**
kiwis 18, 19, 82
　see also kiwi
koala (*Phascolarctos cinereus*) 6, 8, 80
krill 74, **74**

lammergeier (*Gypaetus barbatus*) 53
lechwe (*Kobus lechwe*) 63, **63**
lemming
　Norway (*Lemmus lemmus*) **46**
lemmings 46, 48
　see also lemming
lemur
　Ring-tailed (*Lemur catta*) **6**, **82**
lemurs 82
　see also lemur
leopard
　Clouded (*Neofelis nebulosa*) 6, 17
　Snow (*Panthera uncia*) 6, 52
leopards **51**
　see also leopard
limpet
　Common (*Patella vulgata*) 72

limpets 72, **72**
see also limpet
lion (*Panthera leo*) 39, 41
Mountain *see* puma
lizard
Shingle-backed
(*Trachydosaurus
rugosus*) **37**
Western collared
(*Chrotaphytus collaris*) **29**
loosejaw (*Malacosteus niger*)
77
lugworms 73
lynx (*Felis lynx*) 26,27

macaque
Japanese (*Macaca fuscata*)
23
macaws 17
mackerel (*Scomber
scombrus*) 74
manatee (*Trichechus
manatus*) 56, **56**
maneater *see* shark, Great
white
mara (genus *Dolichotis*) 44
marmosets 9
marmot
Alpine (*Marmota marmota*)
50
marmots 53
see also marmot
marsupials 80
martens 19, **24**, 26, **27**
mayfly (*Cloen dipterum*) 55,
58, 60
mice
Pocket 35
see also mouse
mink
American (*Mustela vison*)
63
moa 82
mole
American shrew
(*Neurotrichus gibbsi*) **18**
Marsupial (*Notoryctes
typhlops*) **35**, 81
moles 19, 22, 88
see also mole
molluscs 55, 58, 60, 69, 71,
72, 73, 79
monkey
Proboscis (*Nasalis larvatus*)
69
monkeys 17,69
Howler 9, **15**
New World 9, **15**, 17
Old World 9
spider 9
see also monkey

moorhen
Gray (*Gallinula chloropus*)
58
moorhens 56, 58, 88
see also moorhen
moose (*Alces alces*) 26
mosquitoes 49, 60, 65
moths 22, 27
mouse
Harvest (*Micromys
minutus*) 84, **84**, 85
House (*Mus musculus*) 88,
88
mudskipper (*Periophthalmus*
species) 69, **69**
muskrat (*Ondata zibethicus*)
63, 65
mussels 55,70,72
newts 60,64

octopus (*octopus* species) 79
opossum
virginia (*Didelphis
virginiana*) **84**
Woolly (*Caluromys lanatus*)
6
opossums 8, 86
common 80
mouse 80
see also opossum
orang-utan (*Pongo
pygmaeus*) **7**, 11
osprey (*Pandion haliaetus*) 64
ostrich (*Struthio camelus*) **32**,
37
otters 56
(genus *Lutra*)
owl
Burrowing (*Athene
cunicularia*) **41**, **44**
Snowy (*Nictea Scandiaca*)
48
owls **33**
see also owl
ox
Musk (*Ovibos moschatus*)
46, **46**
oystercatcher (*Haematopus
ostralegus*) 66

pademelon
Red-bellied (*Thylogale
billardieri*) 19
panda
Giant (*Ailuropoda
melanoleuca*) 7, 9
parrots 17
partridge
Red-legged (*Alectoris rufa*)
84

peccary
Collared (*Tayassu tajacu*)
29
pelicans 88
penguins 79
perch (*Perca fluviatilis*) **58**
pigeon
Feral (*Columba livia*) 87, **89**
pigs, wild 22
pike
Northern (*Esox lucius*) **61**
pikes 58, 60
see also pike
plaice (genus *Pleuronectes*)
79
platypus
Duck-billed (*Ornithorhynchus
anatinus*) 8, 80
porcupine
African (*Hystrix cristata*) **35**
North American (*Erethizon
dorsatum*) **18**
porcupines 9
see also porcupine
porpoises 76, 79
possum
Scaly-tailed (*Wyulda
squamicaudata*) **7**
possums 8
see also possum
prairie dogs (genus *Cynomys*)
42, 44, **44**
pronghorn (*Antilocapra
americana*) **6**, 9, **43**, 44
protozoans 60
ptarmigan (*Lagopus leucurus*)
53
puma (*Felis concolor*) **28**, 30,
35, 52, **53**

quoll
Tasmanian tiger (*Thylacinus
cynocephalus*) 19

rabbit (*Oryctolagus cuniculus*)
66
Swamp (*Sylvilagus
aquaticus*) 63
raccoon
Common (*Procyon lotor*) **88**
raccoons 86
see also raccoon
ragworm (*Nereis diversicolor*)
71, 73
rat
Cane (*Thryonomys
gregorianus*) **84**
Norway (*Rattus norvegicus*)
88
rats 86,88
see also rat

rattlesnakes 37, 44
rays
manta 76
redshank (*Tringa totanus*) 66
reindeer *see* caribou
rhea
Common (*Rhea americana*)
44
rhinoceros
Javan (*Rhinoceros
sondaicus*) 11
White (*Ceratotherium
simum*) 11
rhinoceroses 9
see also rhinoceros
road runner (*Geococcyx
californianus*) **29**, 30
rorquals **79**
rotifers 60

salamanders 64
salmon
Atlantic (*Salmo salar*) 55
sandhoppers (eg *Orchestia
gammarella, Talitrus
saltator*) **71**, 73
Sand mason (*Lanice
conchilega*) **71**
sandpiper
Sharp-tailed (*Calidris
acuminata*) 66
sandpipers 73
see also sandpiper
scorpions 14, **32**, **35**
sea anemones 72, 74, **74**
seal
Cape fur (*Arcocephalus
pusillus*) **78**
Harbor (*Phoca vitulina*) **78**
Ringed (*Phoca hispida*) 48
sea lions 79
seals 12,48,76,79
see also seal
sea potato (*Echinocardium
cordatum*) **71**
sea slugs **76**
sea urchins 72
shark
Great white (*Carcharodon
carcharias*) 76, **76**
Tiger (*Galescerdo cuvier*)
76
sharks 76
basking 76
see also shark
sheep 37, 52
Dall's (*Ovis dalli*) 51
shelduck
Ruddy (*Tadorna ferruginea*)
64

shell
  Common otter (*Lutraria lutraria*) **71**
  Pod razor (*Ensis siliqua*) **71**
shrews 22
shrimps 60,72
  Freshwater (*Gammarus pulex*) 55
sidewinder (*Crotalus cerastes*) **29**
sitatunga (*Tragelaphus spekei*) 63
skua *see* jaeger
sloth 17
  Brown-throated three-toed (*Bradypus variegatus*) **6, 15**
  Giant 9
snail
  Great pond (*Limnea stagnalis*) **58**, 60
snails
  water 55, 60
snakebird *see* darter
snakes 64
souslik (genus *Spermophilus*) 44
sparrow
  House (*Passer domesticus*) 88, **89**
spiders 14,22
  water 54
sponges 79
spoonbill
  Roseate (*Platalea ajaja*) **59**, 64
springtails 19
squid 74
squirrel
  Cape ground (*Xerus inaurus*) **35**
  Douglas (*Tamiasciurus douglasii*) **18**
  Gray (*Sciurus carolinensis*) **21, 87**
  Red (*Sciurus vulgaris*) 24, **24**, 26
squirrels 22, 88
  ground 30, 35, 44, 53
  see also squirrel
starfish
  Common (*Asterias rubens*) 70, 72
starling
  Common (*Sturnus vulgaris*) **89**
stickleback 60
stint 66
  Little (*Calidris minuta*) 66
stoat (*Mustela erminea*) 48
stork
  Marabou (*Leptoptilos crumeniferus*) **40**, 87

swan
  Mute (*Cygnus olor*) **54**
swans 56
  see also swan

takahe (*Notoruis mantelli*) 82, **82**
tamandua
  Southern (*Tamandua tetradactyla*) **41**
tapirs 17
teal
  Marbled (*Marmaronetta angustirostris*) **64**
tellins (eg *Tellina tenuis, Tellina fabula*) **71**
termites 40
tern
  Arctic (*Sterna paradisaea*) 49
  Whiskered (*Chlidonias hybrida*) **64**
thrush
  Song (*Turdus philomelos*) **89**
tit
  coal (*Parus ater*) **21**
tits 22
  see also tit
toad
  Common (*Bufo bufo*) **62**
toads **62**, 63
  see also toad
tortoise
  Giant (*Geochelone elephantophus*) 81,82
toucans 17
tree-shrew
  Terrestrial (*Lynogale tana*) **7**
trout
  Brown (*Salmo trutta*) **56**
  Sea or Salmon *see* trout, Brown
tuco-tuco (genus *Clenomys*) 44

vicuna (*Vicugna vicugna*) **52**
viper
  Common sand (*Cerastes vipera*) **34**
viperfish (*Chauliodus sloani*) 77
viscacha
  Plains (*Lagostomus maximus*) 44
vole
  European water (*Arvicola terrestris*) **58**
voles 88
  water 56
  see also vole

vulture
  Asian white-backed (*Gyps bengalensis*) 84
  Egyptian (*Neophron percnopterus*) 37
  Black (*Coragyps atratus*) 87
vultures 37
  see also vulture

wallabies 19,30
walrus (*Odobenus rosmarus*) 12, **78**, 79
wapiti see deer, Red
warbler
  Arctic (*Phylloscopus borealis*) 49
  Great reed (*Acrocephalus arundinaceus*) **64**
  Paddyfield (*A. agricola*) **84**
  Sedge (*A. schoenobaenus*) **58**
  Willow (*Phylloscopus trochilus*) 22
wasps
  gall (eg *Biorrhiza pallida*) 21
  spangle gall 23
weasels 9, 44
whale
  Blue (*Balaenoptera musculus*) 79
  Humpback (*Megaptera novaeangliae*) **79**
  Killer (*Orcinus orca*) 79
  Right (*Balaena glacialis*) 79
  Sperm (*Physter macrocephalus*) 79
whalefish (*Cetominus indagator*) 77
whales 79
  baleen **74**, 76, 79
  see also whale
whelk
  Dog (*Nucella lapillus*) 72
whelks 72
  see also whelk
wild dog
  African (*Lycaeon pictus*) 41
wild dogs 41
  see also wild dog
wildebeest 38,40
winkle
  Mangrove (*Littorina scabra*) **69**
winkles 72
  see also winkle
wisent *see* bison, European
wolf
  Gray (*Canis lupus*) **49**
  Tasmanian (*Thylacinus cynocephalus*) 81
wolverine (*Gulo gulo*) 27, 48

wolves 26, 30, 44, 48, 52
  see also wolf
woodlice 19, 22
worm
  Peacock (*Sabella pavonina*) **71**
worms 20, 22, 55, 58, 60, 66, 69
  fan 73
  flat 58
  polychaete (*Nephtys caeca, Amphitrite johnstoni*) **71**, 73,79
  see also worm

zebra
  Plains (*Equus burchelli*) 40
zebras 38, **38**, 40, 41
  see also zebra
zooplankton 60

FURTHER READING

Berry, R. J. (1977), *Inheritance and Natural History*, Collins, London.

Blondel, J. (1979), *Biographie et écologie.* Masson, Paris.

Carlquist, S. (1974), *Island Biology*, Columbia, New York.

Chapman, V. J. (ed) (1977), *Wet Coastal Ecosystems (Ecosystems of the World*, vol 1), Elsevier, New York.

Chernov, Y. I. (1985), *The Living Tundra*, Cambridge University Press, Cambridge

Cloudsley-Thompson, J. I. (1984), *Sahara Desert*, Pergamon Press, Oxford.

Collinson, A. S. (1977), *Introduction to World Vegetation*, George Allen and Unwin, London.

Cox, C. B and Moore, P. D. (1985), *Biogeography: An Ecological and Evolutionary Approach* (4th edition), Blackwell Scientific Publications, Oxford.

Ehrlich, P. R., Ehrlich, A. H. and Holdren, J. P. (1977), *Ecoscience: Population, Resources, Environment*, W. H. Freeman, San Francisco.

Heywood, V. H. (ed) (1985), *Flowering Plants of the World*, Croom Helm, London.

Hora, B. (ed) (1981), *Oxford Encyclopedia of Trees of the World*, Oxford University Press, Oxford.

Krebs, C. J. (1985), *Ecology* (3rd edition) Harper and Row, New York.

May, R.M. (ed) (1976), *Theoretical Ecology*, Blackwell, Oxford.

Moore, P. D. M. (ed) (1982), *Green Planet: The Story of Plant Life on Earth*, Cambridge University Press, Cambridge.

Moore, P. D. M. (ed) (1986), *The Encyclopedia of Animal Ecology*, Facts on File, New York.

Myers, N. (1984), *The Primary Source: Tropical Forests and Our Future*, Norton, New York.

Pielou, E. C. (1979), *Biogeography*, John Wiley, New York.

Polunin, O. and Walters, M. (1985), *A Guide to the Vegetation of Britain and Europe*, Oxford University Press, Oxford.

Putman R. J. and Wratten, S. D. (1984), *Principles of Ecology*, Croom Helm, London.

Scott, P. (ed) (1974), *The World Atlas of Birds*, Mitchell Beazley, London.

Simon J. I. and Kahn, H. (eds) (1984), *The Resourceful Earth*, Basil Blackwell, Oxford

Sutton, S. L. Whitmore, T. C. and Chadwick, A. C. (1983), *Tropical Rain Forest: Ecology and Management.* Blackwell Scientific Publications, Oxford.

Tudge, C. (1988), *The Environment of Life*, Oxford University Press, New York.

Walter, H. (1979), *Vegetation of the Earth*, Springer-Verlag, New York.

Whittaker, R. H. (1975), *Communities and Ecosystems*, Collier Macmillan, London.

Young, J. Z. (1981) *The Life of Vertebrates* (£rd edn.), Clarendon, England.

ACKNOWLEDGMENTS

Picture credits

Key: t top, b bottom, c center, l left, r right.
Abbreviations: AN Agence Nature, ANT Australian Nature Transparencies, BCL Bruce CColeman Ltd, NHPA Natural History Photographic Agency, OSF Oxford Scientific Films, P. Premaphotos Wildlife, PEP Planet Earth Pictures. SAL Survival Anglia Ltd, SPL Science Photo Library.

4 Frans Lanting. 6-7 Denys Ovenden. 7 F.E. Beaton. 8 Hayward Art Group. 9 Andrew Laurie. 10tr Hayward Art Group. 10b Wayne Ford. 11 George Frame. 12 PEP/R. Salm. 13 Hayward Art Group. 14t Biofotos/S. Summerhays. 14b Hayward Art Group. 15 Michael Fogden. 16 Graham Allen. 17 Auscape International/G. Threlfo. 18b Hayward Art Group. 18-19 Denys Ovenden. 19 Ardea. 20 Hayward Art Group. 20-21 Ardea. 21t OSF. 21b P. 22bl David Hosking. 22br Jacana/F. Winner. 23t BCL/A.J. Deane. 23b Ardea/F. Gohier. 24t J. Kaufmann. 24b Hayward Art Group. 25l Aquila. 25r Ardea/S. Roberts. 26-27 Denys Ovenden. 28t OSF. 28b Hayward Art Group. 29 Denys Ovenden. 31 ANT/T. and P. Gardner. 32t PEP/Sean Avery. 32b Hayward Art Group. 33tl Natural Science Photos/Dick Brown. 33tr Agence Nature. 33b BCL. 34l NHPA/S. Dalton. 34-35 Denys Ovenden. 35t OSF. 36 C.A. Henley. 38t Jacana/Arthus-Bertrand. 38b Hayward Art Group. 39t OSF/Kathy Tyrrell. 39b SAL/Alan Root. 40 Michael Fogden. 41l Denys Ovenden. 41r P/K. Preston-Mafham. 42t SAL/Jeff Foott. 43t BCL. 43b, 44-45 W. Ervin, Natural Imagery. 46t NHPA/S.Kraseman. 46b Priscilla Barrett. 47t Hayward Art Group. 47b Jacana. 48 OSF/M. Carlisle. 49t Fred Bruemmer. 49b Jacana. 50b Hayward Art Group. 50-51 Denys Ovenden. 52t Frank Picture Lane Agency/Silvestris. 52b BCL/R. Peterson. 53 NHPA/S. Kraseman. 54tr SAL. 54bl NHPA/M. Danegger. 54br OSF/J.A.L. Cooke. 55 PEP/N. Downer. 56 Sirenia Project, DWRC Florida. 57 Biofotos/Heather Angel. 58-59 Denys Ovenden. 59 BCL. 60t NHPA/M. Walker. 60b Biofotos/H. Angel. 60-61 Mick Saunders. 61b PEP/K. Cullimore.62t Biofotos/H. Angel. 62-63 A. Bannister. 63 Frank Lane Picture Agency/Fritz Polking. 64-65 Denys Ovenden. 66 G.R. Roberts. 66-67 Swift Picture Library/Mike Read. 67 Ardea. 68-69 Mick Loates. 70-71 Roger Gorringe. 72t E. & D. Hosking/D.P. Wilson. 72b A. Bannister. 72-73 Mick Saunders. 73 Biofotos/H. Angel. 74t NHPA/P. Johnson. 74b OSF/F. Ehrenstrom. 75 PEP/Bill Wood. 76t PEP/Marty Snyderman. 76b BCL/A. Power. 77 Mick Loates. 78 Priscilla Barrett. 79t Oxford Illustrators Ltd. 79b Ardea/F. Gohier. 80 Zefa/E. Christian. 81t ANT/Tony Howard. 81bl Frank Lane Agency/F. Polking. 81br Priscilla Barrett. 82 ANT/M.F. Soper. 82-83 BCL. 84t A. Bannister. 84-85 Denys Ovenden. 86 D.W. Macdonald. 86-87 NHPA/M. Leach. 87 OSF. 88-89 Denys Ovenden. 89 Frank Lane Picture Agency/A.R. Hamblin.

Artwork © Priscilla Barrett 1986